GOD'S VICTORY PLAN

God's Victory Plan

Kenneth Hagin Jr.

Unless otherwise indicated, all Scripture quotations in this volume are from the *King James Version* of the Bible.

First Printing 1994

ISBN 0-89276-731-6

In the U.S. write:
Kenneth Hagin Ministries
P.O. Box 50126
Tulsa, OK 74150-0126

In Canada write:
Kenneth Hagin Ministries
P.O. Box 335
Etobicoke (Toronto), Ontario
Canada, M9A 4X3

BOOKS BY KENNETH E. HAGIN

Following God's Plan For Your Life
The Triumphant Church
Healing Scriptures
Mountain Moving Faith
The Price Is Not Greater Than God's Grace (Mrs. Oretha Hagin)

MINIBOOKS (A partial listing)

* *The New Birth*
* *Why Tongues?*
* *In Him*
* *God's Medicine*
* *You Can Have What You Say*
   How To Write Your Own Ticket With God
* *Don't Blame God*
* *Words*
   Plead Your Case
* *How To Keep Your Healing*
   The Bible Way To Receive the Holy Spirit
   I Went to Hell
   How To Walk in Love
   The Precious Blood of Jesus
* *Love Never Fails*
   Your Faith in God Will Work

BOOKS BY KENNETH HAGIN JR.

* *Man's Impossibility — God's Possibility*
   Because of Jesus
   How To Make the Dream God Gave You Come True
   The Life of Obedience
   God's Irresistible Word
   Healing: Forever Settled
   Don't Quit! Your Faith Will See You Through
   The Untapped Power in Praise
   Listen to Your Heart
   What Comes After Faith?
   Speak to Your Mountain!
   Come Out of the Valley

MINIBOOKS (A partial listing)

* *Faith Worketh by Love*
   Blueprint for Building Strong Faith
* *Seven Hindrances to Healing*
* *The Past Tense of God's Word*
   Faith Takes Back What the Devil's Stolen
   "The Prison Door Is Open — What Are You Still Doing Inside?"
   How To Be a Success in Life
   Get Acquainted With God
   Showdown With the Devil
   Unforgiveness
   Ministering to the Brokenhearted

*These titles are also available in Spanish. Information about other foreign translations of several of the above titles (i.e., Finnish, French, German, Indonesian, Polish, Russian, etc.) may be obtained by writing to: Kenneth Hagin Ministries, P.O. Box 50126, Tulsa, Oklahoma 74150-0126.

Contents

Contents

Chapter 1
Following God's Plan Brings Victory

From eternity past into the timeless eternity that is to come, God has had a plan. God is a God of purpose, and He forms His plans to fulfill His divine purposes for His creation.

The Word of God records God's great plan of redemption for all of mankind. And it also records many of God's plans for individual people and nations.

As you study the Word, you'll find that all of God's plans bring victory. In fact, you will never find one time where *God's* plan failed. God makes plans that will succeed. Never once has God organized anything that wasn't designed to bring victory.

We need to understand that when God tells us to do something a certain way, it is part of His plan to bring us victory. He does *not* intend for His plan to fail. The only way God's plan can fail is if *we* fail to execute His plan the way He told us to do it.

We can see the truth of this principle even in the natural realm. For instance, one season I was watching the national basketball playoffs on television. One of

1

the coaches was discussing a basketball game his team had played the day before against a tough opponent.

The winning record of the opposing team was so much greater than this coach's team that it was surprising the two teams were even playing against each other. But this coach's team won — the underdog team — and this coach was explaining why.

The coach said, "In the second half of the game, my team finally played the game according to the plan I had drawn up in the locker room."

Once this basketball team began to execute the coach's plan, the team began to score points. And they won the game even though the other team they were playing was supposed to be a much better team.

That's the way it is in sports. One team can actually be made up of better athletes, but if the players don't execute the proper plan on the court or field, they'll lose the game.

The same thing can happen in the spiritual realm. When believers don't execute God's plan in their lives, Satan is able to steal the victory that is rightfully theirs in Christ.

If believers are not living their lives according to God's plan, they cannot claim the victory God promises them as the outcome of His plan. And it won't be because of God! It will be because they failed to execute *God's* plan.

When we were building the new RHEMA Bible Church auditorium, I would often go out on the new building site and walk around to look at all the construction. I could see those steel beams towering into the air and the steel girders that went down deep into the ground.

Even in the natural in construction, everything has to be executed according to the plan the engineer draws up, or it won't work. If the building contractor doesn't follow the blueprint exactly, those huge steel beams won't fit together properly. When you have a set of plans, but don't build according to the plans, something isn't going to work out right!

What do you think a car would look like if the engineers drew up a plan showing exactly what the car was supposed to look like, but then the men on the assembly line decided they were going to build the car any way they wanted to. I can guarantee that a car built like that would come off the assembly line a mess! It's liable to end up with a fender on top, no wheels, and the motor in the trunk!

You see, when the engineers drew up the plans for assembling a new car, they designed it according to certain specifications. And each time that car moves down the assembly line to a different station, other parts are added to it according to the plan.

When that car finally rolls out the door at the other end of the assembly line, it's a completed automobile. And it exactly matches the engineers' specifications.

When I was a kid living down in Garland, Texas, they used to have a big Ford car manufacturing plant in Dallas, Texas, which wasn't far from where we lived. The grade-school teachers used to take us on field trips to that plant. It was a big deal for us to go on a field trip to the Ford plant and watch the men on the assembly line put a Ford station wagon together.

In fact, my class visited the Ford plant in 1949, and we watched them assemble a '49 Ford station wagon. If you remember, that was the one with the real wood panels on the side.

In those days, everything was done by man. Now most of the work is automated. But back then, each man on that assembly line had his own particular job in assembling a car.

When the station wagon first started down the assembly line, it was just a plain steel frame. At the first station, one man bolted parts onto the car. Then it passed down the assembly line to the next station where other parts were supplied.

By the time that station wagon had finished moving through the assembly line, the entire car had been built. At the end of the assembly line, it was one man's job to put two gallons of gasoline in the car so they could drive it off the assembly line and onto the parking lot.

When that station wagon finally rolled off the assembly line, it was completely finished — gasoline and all — and a man got in, drove it off the assembly line, and parked it!

But it wouldn't have been possible to build that car unless the Ford plant had a plan for manufacturing cars. The plan was complete from A to Z. And because the plan was carried out to perfection, thousands of cars were produced and sold — all as a result of following just one plan.

If the Ford plant can produce successful cars from a plan, how much more do you suppose we can win the victory with God's plans for us, His very own children? God already knows the plans that will bring each of us victory, but it's up to us to follow them according to His specifications!

God's Triumph Over Jericho

Let's look at some examples of God's victory plans in the Bible. In Joshua chapter 5, the captain of the Lord's hosts appeared to Joshua. God wanted to reveal His plan to Joshua. It was a plan that would allow the Israelites to triumph over Jericho, a strong fortified city. No one had ever been able to defeat Jericho.

> **JOSHUA 5:13,14**
> 13 And it came to pass, when Joshua was by Jericho, that he lifted up his eyes and looked, and, behold, THERE STOOD A MAN OVER AGAINST HIM WITH HIS SWORD DRAWN IN HIS HAND: and Joshua went unto him, and said unto him, Art thou for us, or for our adversaries?
> 14 And he said, Nay; but as captain of the host of the Lord am I now come. And Joshua fell on his face to the earth, and did worship, and said unto him, What saith my lord unto his servant?

Joshua didn't know who this Man was at first. He didn't know if He was a friend or a foe. That's why Joshua asked Him, "Are you for us or against us?"

The Man answered, "I'm the Captain of the Lord's host."

When the Captain of the Lord's host said that, Joshua immediately recognized that God had sent His Captain to help Joshua fight the enemy in Jericho. Notice Joshua's first question: "*. . . What saith my lord unto his servant?*" In other words, the first thing Joshua asked Him was this: "What's the plan?"

Instead of answering Joshua right away, the Captain of the Lord's host told Joshua, "Take off your shoes. The ground you're standing on is holy."

JOSHUA 5:15
15 And the captain of the Lord's host said unto Joshua, Loose thy shoe from off thy foot; for the place whereon thou standest is holy. And Joshua did so.

What was He telling Joshua? In effect, He was saying, "Joshua, you are dealing with the holiness of God. I'm about to reveal the plan of God to you, and it is holy too. So don't treat the plan of God as a light thing and be flippant about it."

Friend, I want you to realize that when you start getting hold of God's victory plan, you're not to treat it flippantly. You can't just run off with it, think you can make a few confessions over it, and carry it out in your own strength. It is a holy thing! And it will require God's strength and wisdom to carry it off.

It's holy because it is God's plan. It is not something that you can just pass off lightly. Respect it as holy because it's *God*'s plan! And it will only produce victory if *you* don't change it!

Then the Lord revealed His victory plan in detail to Joshua for taking Jericho.

JOSHUA 6:2-5
2 And the Lord said unto Joshua, See, I have given into thine hand Jericho, and the king thereof, and the mighty man of valour.
3 And ye shall compass the city, all ye men of war, and go round about the city once. Thus shalt thou do six days.
4 And SEVEN priests shall bear before the ark SEVEN trumpets of rams' horns: and the SEVENTH day ye shall compass the city SEVEN times, and the priests shall blow with the trumpets.
5 And it shall come to pass, that when they make a long blast with the ram's horn, and when ye hear the sound of the trumpet, ALL THE PEOPLE SHALL SHOUT WITH A GREAT SHOUT; and the wall of the city shall fall down flat, and the people shall ascend up every man straight before him.

In this passage, God gave the Israelites a detailed plan for conquering Jericho. But the Israelites had to carry it out according to God's exact specifications, or it wouldn't work.

For example, notice that God said *seven* priests were to carry the ark. That was an exact detail of the plan of God, wasn't it? But what if some of the Israelites argued, "Yes, but we don't need *seven* to carry it. Six will do just fine"?

What man thinks about God's plan doesn't make any difference. *God* said, *"Seven* priests shall carry the ark," so that's the way it was supposed to be done.

God also said that *seven* priests were to blow *seven* trumpets of rams' horns. The Israelites could have argued, "But we only have six priests who know how to blow the rams' horns."

Well, you'd better find another priest then, because God said there were to be *seven*. God has a purpose for everything in His plan, and He expects His people to execute His plan exactly as He instructs them.

So many times God tells us to do something through His Word and by His Holy Spirit, and in our hearts we answer, "But, Lord, I want to do it *my* way!" However, when God is telling us to do something, we have no right to say, "But, Lord . . ." God knows *His* plan will bring us victory, not *ours*.

God's plan is not something to treat flippantly by changing it if we don't like it. Once we get God's plan, we can't just ignore what He tells us to do. We also can't take what He tells us, mouth a bunch of confessions about victory, and then run off and try to accomplish His plan in our own strength.

Once you know what God's plan is, you'll have to determine to obey Him and to follow His plan completely. That's how success comes. That's when there's victory.

But you'll never experience victory when you just follow part of God's plan — the part you like. You've got to follow God's victory plan completely.

You need to make this decision: "I *will* follow God completely. I will not let my own opinions get in the way." Only *you* can make that decision.

Then be sure you do it! That's the only way you'll walk in the victory God has prepared for you!

God gave Joshua all the details to carry out His plan. God will do the same thing for you and me if we will seek Him for His plan. He will give us each step to fulfill His plan.

Then Joshua rehearsed the Lord's plan to all the Israelites so they would know exactly what the Lord required of them.

JOSHUA 6:6-10
6 And Joshua the son of Nun called the priests, and said unto them, Take up the ark of the covenant, and let seven priests bear seven trumpets of rams' horns before the ark of the Lord.
7 And he said unto the people, Pass on, and compass the city, and let him that is armed pass on before the ark of the Lord.
8 And it came to pass, when Joshua had spoken unto the people, that the seven priests bearing the seven trumpets of rams' horns passed on before the Lord, and blew with the trumpets: and the ark of the covenant of the Lord followed them.
9 And the armed men went before the priests that blew with the trumpets, and the rereward came after the ark, the priests going on, and blowing with the trumpets.
10 And Joshua had commanded the people, saying, Ye shall not shout, nor make any noise with your voice, neither shall any word proceed out of your mouth, until the day I bid you shout; then shall ye shout.

Notice that the only instruction the armed men were given was to march on ahead of the Ark of the Covenant (v. 7).

I imagine it was hard for trained fighting men just to march and not charge into battle. However, if they hadn't obeyed that instruction completely, the plan would have ended in failure.

Know When To Be Silent

Then according to the Lord's instructions, Joshua told the people not to shout or make any noise at all (v. 10).

In fact, not one word was to proceed out of their mouths until the day that Joshua gave the instruction to shout.

That's an unusual instruction, isn't it? Those Israelites could have thought, *That doesn't make any sense! There's no reason we need to do that!* But God had a reason for telling them that.

He knew that if they started talking, they'd talk themselves right out of faith into doubt and unbelief!

Some of us are marching in the direction God told us to go, all right. But our mouths are open, and we're just spewing out negative words all the time. Those words are putting up roadblocks to our being able to fulfill the plan of God.

All we're doing is complaining about what God told us to do. God is trying to get us to shut our mouths, so we can stand in faith for His plan! Victory will never come by complaining.

Some people say, "Oh, but I am standing for God!" They may think they are, but their mouths are going so fast that their negative words negate what they're standing for!

I think it was the same way with these Israelites. God knew if He let them talk, their mouths would get them into defeat. They would talk themselves right out of faith.

> **JOSHUA 6:11**
> **11 So the ark of the Lord compassed the city, going about it once: and they came into the camp, and LODGED IN THE CAMP.**

You see, God even gave the Israelites time to rest and lounge around at the camp every evening. He's not a hard taskmaster. He didn't just drive them all the time to accomplish His purposes. His plan isn't too hard to obey.

The Bible says the Lord watches over His people to give them rest, and He leads them like a shepherd would his own flock (Ps. 23:1-6). God doesn't make His plan impossible to accomplish.

The Shout of Victory!

Now let's see what happened on the seventh day. God had a specific plan for that day, down to every detail.

JOSHUA 6:14-16
14 And the second day they compassed the city once, and returned into the camp: so they did six days.
15 And it came to pass on the seventh day, that they rose early about the dawning of the day, and compassed the city after the same manner seven times: only on that day they compassed the city seven times.
16 And it came to pass at the seventh time, when the priests blew with the trumpets, Joshua said unto the people, Shout; for the Lord hath given you the city.

I want you to notice something. The Israelites had surrounded the city for six days. Then on the seventh day, the priests were supposed to blow the trumpets and the people were supposed to shout the victory.

Why did God tell the people to shout? Because the Lord had promised to give the Israelites the city, so the people were to act in faith by shouting the victory *before* the walls came down.

Now look at this and learn something about faith. When the priests blew the trumpets, the wall was still standing. When Joshua told the people to shout, the walls were still standing. The people shouted anyway because it was part of God's *plan*. You see, the shout of faith always comes *before* the answer!

What if the Israelites had said, "But I don't feel like shouting, Joshua." Then nothing would have happened. God's victory plan wouldn't have been carried out, so the Israelites would have been defeated.

You see, sometimes the Lord tells us to shout the victory in faith *before* we see the victory. Sometimes He tells us to shout in victory even when we don't feel like it. Feelings have nothing to do with it.

We're supposed to go ahead and shout the victory in faith, regardless of what we *see* or *feel*. God never told us we had to *feel* the victory; He just told us to *act out* the victory in faith.

Get ahold of this faith principle. It wasn't until the Israelites began shouting that the walls started tumbling down. You see, the Israelites were acting out their faith — they were shouting while the walls were still standing.

Are you shouting the victory in faith while your walls are still standing? You may have walls of opposition, walls of hindrance, or walls of impossibility. But that's why God wants you to shout in victory! He knows faith in Him is what will bring those walls down.

It was part of God's victory plan for the Israelites to shout in victory while the walls were still standing, and it worked. I'm sure it probably didn't make sense to them. But all they had to do was obey God and do it God's way.

From God's instructions to the Israelites here at Jericho, we can see two principles in following God's victory plan in our own lives.

The first thing to do is to *find out God's plan*. The next thing is to *carry it out exactly like God said it*.

How do you determine God's plan? First, you have to listen to what God says by studying His Word. Then you've got to listen for the Holy Spirit's leading in your own spirit. He will show you exactly how to walk out His plan.

God's Word Is God's Plan

In the Old Testament, God often sent a messenger — sometimes an angel or a prophet — to relay His plan to His people. But under the New Covenant, we don't need angels or prophets to tell us God's plan.

We have the written Word of God to instruct us and the Holy Spirit dwelling within us to guide and direct us (2 Tim. 3:16; Rom. 8:14).

Some people today are always running around looking for a word from the Lord when they are carrying an entire collection of God's words — the Bible — under their arm!

When they find someone they think is spiritual, they ask, "Brother, could you give me a word from the Lord?" Their Christian brother should tell them, "You've got God's Word inside the covers of that Book you're carrying. Find out what God says in that Book and then *do* it."

If you said that to some people, they'd say, "Oh, man, I don't want to do that! That's too hard."

God never promised it would always be easy to obey Him. But He did promise that we would always walk in victory if we would follow His plan for our lives: *"Now thanks be unto God, which ALWAYS CAUSETH US TO TRIUMPH IN CHRIST. . ."* (2 Cor. 2:14).

God intends for the victory — His victory plan — to be ours in every circumstance.

1 CORINTHIANS 15:57
57 But thanks be to God, WHICH GIVETH US THE VICTORY through our Lord Jesus Christ.

God didn't promise us that we would never have tests or trials. But He did promise that He would deliver us out of every one of them!

PSALM 34:17,19
17 The righteous cry, and the Lord heareth, and DELIVERETH THEM OUT OF ALL THEIR TROUBLES. . . .
19 Many are the afflictions of the righteous: but the Lord delivereth him OUT OF THEM ALL.

So let's find out what God's plan is, and do it His way, not our way. Victories come by doing what God says.

When we begin to follow God and do what God says, sometimes what God tells us to do might seem utterly foolish and inadequate to the human mind — like shouting in victory while the walls are still standing.

God's instructions may seem like they won't work. But, actually, God is just trying to get us into faith and obedience, because if we do what *God* said to do, it will work — every single time.

Think how foolish God's plan to take Jericho must have seemed to the Israelites. The walls surrounding Jericho were so formidable, no one had ever been able to capture the city.

But did God tell the Israelites to storm the walls with all their military force? No, He told them to do something that didn't make any sense to the natural mind.

He only told them to march around the city for seven days, then shout the victory on the last day. Does that make any sense to the human mind? No!

How can an army take a city by marching around it for seven days? And how can a blast from trumpets and loud shouts make thick walls crash and fall?

In the natural, that would be impossible. But when God says, "It will happen because it is *My* plan," then victory *will* come. God's plan *will* be accomplished.

When the Israelites obeyed God's plan for victory exactly as He had instructed them, the walls of Jericho came tumbling down with a mighty "Thud!" and the city was conquered.

You won't always understand God's plan with your natural reasoning. Sometimes God's plan will seem utterly ridiculous to your mind or to other people.

But we've got to realize that we don't answer to humans; we answer to *God*. What His plan looks like, sounds like, or feels like has nothing to do with its ultimate outcome. His plan will never contradict His Word. But if God said to do it, the outcome will be victory!

I remember a certain minister who began his ministry in a little church on the bad side of town. Dad held a crusade for that pastor when I was his crusade director. The church was so small that we had to stuff people everywhere we could — behind the platform, on the platform, in the balcony.

That was the smallest church I'd ever seen. The balcony held ten people. By stuffing people everywhere, we finally sat 300 people. We had a three-foot-square book table, and when we piled our books on it, it seemed like it almost filled the whole room!

But that pastor just kept following God's victory plan for his church, and the congregation continued to grow. Then after a few years, that congregation wanted a certain property because they needed to build a bigger church building.

At the time, they didn't have any money to buy a church building. In the natural, it looked ridiculous to claim a building by faith. But that's exactly what that congregation did.

They walked around a certain property in faith, claiming it for the Lord. And miraculously they were able to buy that property!

Later that same congregation bought a huge facility, which is now debt-free! They were able to do that because step by step they followed God's plan — not man's.

I'm sure when they claimed both those properties, they probably felt inadequate, knowing that they didn't have any money. But it doesn't matter how foolish it seems to the human brain, if God said to do it, then do it! Besides, if it's really God who is talking to you, it will line up with the Word and it will bring results.

Several years ago during a prayer meeting on the RHEMA campus, we marched all over the campus, praying for the various outreaches of this ministry. It probably looked stupid for a group of people to be out marching and praying around this campus. But God said to do it, so we did it!

Since then we've been able to look back to that time and see many things that took place as a result of that time of prayer.

One interesting thing that happened was that at the time, we were having trouble maintaining our duck population in the RHEMA pond. As we walked by the duck pond, we just said, "Lord, replenish the ducks." After that, we had more ducks than we knew what to do with!

What I'm saying to you is that sometimes what you see in the Word of God and what God is telling you to do seems utterly ridiculous to the human mind. But just remember — God knows how to bring His victory plan to pass!

Victory comes when you follow God's plan completely. Just rely on God to perform the supernatural in your life. You're not responsible for bringing the supernatural to pass in God's plan. Your only responsibility is to *obey* God's plan so *He* can bring it to pass!

Chapter 2
You Are a Mighty Victor In Christ!

In Judges 6, we find another biblical example of God's supernatural victory plan working against all odds. In this passage, we can see how God's plan defies natural circumstances — but it brings victory every time.

Here we find a story about a fellow named Gideon. The angel of the Lord appeared to Gideon to deliver a message to him from God. The angel said that God had chosen him to be Israel's deliverer from the Midianites. When the angel spoke to Gideon, the angel hailed him as a "mighty man of valor."

In the natural, the angel's greeting didn't seem to fit Gideon at all. Gideon sure didn't think of himself as a mighty man of valor! In fact, he really didn't agree with God's choice of him as Israel's deliverer. In fact, when the angel came to speak to him, Gideon was hiding out behind the winepress threshing wheat so the Midianites couldn't see him and steal the wheat. He wasn't acting much like a mighty man of valor. He was scared and in hiding.

JUDGES 6:11-15

11 And there came an angel of the Lord, and sat under an oak which was in Ophrah, that pertained unto Joash the Abiezrite: and his son Gideon threshed wheat by the winepress, to hide it from the Midianites.

12 And the angel of the Lord appeared unto him, and said unto him, The Lord is with thee, THOU MIGHTY MAN OF VALOR.

13 And Gideon said unto him, Oh my Lord, if the Lord be with us, why then is all this befallen us? and where be all his miracles which our fathers told us of, saying, Did not the Lord bring us up from Egypt? but now the Lord hath forsaken us, and delivered us into the hands of the Midianites.

14 And the Lord looked upon him, and said, Go in this thy might, and THOU SHALT SAVE ISRAEL FROM THE HAND OF THE MIDIANITES: have not I sent thee?

15 And he said unto him, Oh my Lord, wherewith shall I save Israel? behold, my family is poor in Manasseh, and I AM THE LEAST IN MY FATHER'S HOUSE.

In other words, Gideon told the angel, "How can *I* save the Midianites! You say I'm a mighty man of valor, but I am the least of the least in the entire tribe of Manasseh."

It didn't look like Gideon was a mighty man of valor. Gideon sure didn't *feel* like a mighty warrior. He seemed weak and inadequate to do what God said. And according to human abilities, Gideon was inadequate to lead the Israelites to victory. But not according to God's plan.

You see, God saw Gideon as he would become under the anointing of the Holy Spirit. With the power of the Holy Spirit upon him, Gideon would become a mighty man of valor. Gideon was inadequate in himself just like you and I are. But with the power of God on his life, he was invincible!

The same is true in your life. It doesn't matter if you think you're inadequate for the job God has called you to do. God sees you as a mighty person of valor!

And it doesn't matter what other people think about you either. Maybe you've been held in bondage by other people's opinion of you. But all that counts is what *God* says about you. When God and you are a team, you can accomplish anything by His mighty power at work through you!

What has God told you to do to bring about His victory plan in your life? If you'll obey God's plan completely, you'll be victorious because God's plan always brings victory!

Get *God's* Instructions!

Gideon found out that obedience to God's plan brings victory — no matter how impossible things seem in the natural realm. God's plan is usually a plan against all odds — that's why it takes the supernatural power of God to do it. So the first thing Gideon had to do to succeed was to find out what God's plan was.

JUDGES 7:1-3
1   Then Jerubbaal, who is Gideon, and all the people that were with him, rose up early, and

**pitched beside the well of Harod: so that the host
of the Midianites were on the north side of them,
by the hill of Moreh, in the valley.
2 And THE LORD SAID UNTO GIDEON, The people that are with thee are too many for me to give
the Midianites into their hands, lest Israel vaunt
themselves against me, saying, Mine own hand
hath saved me.
3 Now therefore go to, proclaim in the ears of the
people, saying, Whosoever is fearful and afraid, let
him return and depart early from mount Gilead.
And there returned of the people twenty and two
thousand; and there remained ten thousand.**

When Gideon followed the Lord's instructions and
marshalled the forces of Israel, there were 32,000 fighting men. In the natural, it probably wouldn't be hard to
fight a battle with that many soldiers.

But then the Lord did something totally unexpected.
He told Gideon, "That's too many men! If you fight this
battle with all those soldiers, Israel will just say they
fought and won the battle all by themselves!"

So the Lord told Gideon to send all the men home
who were fearful. Gideon obeyed, and the 32,000-strong
Israelite army was reduced to 10,000 men to fight a
major battle (Judges 7:2,3). The Midianites and their
allies were coming against Israel with a great host of
135,000 fighting men (Judges 8:10).

But 10,000 strong fighting men still didn't satisfy
the Lord! Then God told Gideon, ". . . *The people are yet
too many* . . ." (Judges 7:4). You see, God wanted to
show the Israelites what *He* could do.

It's true that 10,000 Israelites would have been fighting against enormous odds in a battle against 135,000 enemy soldiers. But God wanted His people to experience a victory that was undeniably supernatural — against *all* odds.

So God told the Israelites that there were still too many Israelite soldiers! God knew what He was doing! He was working His victory plan. Remember, it's not the arm of flesh that brings the victory. It's God's supernatural power working in the situation that leads to victory every single time!

So God told Gideon to reduce the army again. This time the Lord gave the soldiers another test. Those who lapped water like dogs were chosen to stay and fight the Midianite battle.

JUDGES 7:4-7
4   And the Lord said unto Gideon, THE PEOPLE ARE YET TOO MANY; bring them down unto the water, and I will try them for thee there: and it shall be, that of whom I say unto thee, This shall go with thee, the same shall go with thee; and of whomsoever I say unto thee, This shall not go with thee, the same shall not go.
5   So he brought down the people unto the water: and the Lord said unto Gideon, EVERY ONE THAT LAPPETH OF THE WATER WITH HIS TONGUE, AS A DOG LAPPETH, him shalt thou set by himself; likewise every one that boweth down upon his knees to drink.
6   And THE NUMBER OF THEM THAT LAPPED, putting their hand to their mouth, were THREE HUNDRED MEN: but all the rest of the people bowed down upon their knees to drink water.

> **7   And the Lord said unto Gideon, By the THREE
> HUNDRED MEN that lapped WILL I SAVE YOU,
> and deliver the Midianites into thine hand: and let
> all the other people go every man unto his place.**

Only 300 men were left to fight with Gideon against
the Midianites. It was only then that God said to
Gideon, "Okay, it's time to go to war."

Why did God do it that way? Because then there
was absolutely no hope that *man* could conquer the
enemy in his own strength! God got all the glory.

No one in their right mind would take 300 men
against an army of 135,000. That's less than one percent of the Midianite fighting force! Human reason says
that an army of that size is going to be defeated!

But despite impossible odds, Gideon took his 300
fighting men down into the valley to engage the enemy
in battle. Gideon knew victory would come only if he did
it God's way, so he obeyed God's instructions exactly.

> **JUDGES 7:17-22**
> **17 And he [Gideon] said unto them, Look on me,
> and do likewise: and, behold, when I come to the
> outside of the camp, it shall be that, as I do, so
> shall ye do.**
> **18 When I blow with a trumpet, I and all that are
> with me, then blow ye the trumpets also on every
> side of all the camp, and say, The sword of the
> Lord, and of Gideon.**
> **19 So Gideon, and the hundred men that were
> with him, came unto the outside of the camp in the
> beginning of the middle watch; and they had but**

newly set the watch: and they blew the trumpets, and brake the pitchers that were in their hands.
20 And the three companies blew the trumpets, and brake the pitchers, and held the lamps in their left hands, and the trumpets in their right hands to blow withal: and they cried, The sword of the Lord, and of Gideon.
21 And they stood every man in his place round about the camp: and all the host ran, and cried, and fled.
22 And THE THREE HUNDRED BLEW THE TRUMPETS, and THE LORD SET EVERY MAN'S SWORD AGAINST HIS FELLOW, even throughout all the host: and the host fled. . . .

As it turned out, the Israelite army didn't even have to fight! Believe me, in the natural, the battle plan didn't make any sense! According to the Lord's instructions, the 300 Israelites broke their water pitchers, blew their trumpets, and gave a mighty shout! When they did that, God caused that huge enemy host to be routed and defeated.

The same thing can be true in your life. Do it God's way and most of the time you won't even have to fight! You'll just have to stand your ground on the Word. Just give a shout in Jesus' Name, and the devil will run in terror! He's already been defeated, so walk out your victory in Jesus Christ!

So the first step to walking God's victory plan is to listen to God and determine what His plan is. The second step is to wait on God for His timing. The third step is to carry out His plan *exactly*.

Learn To Wait on God's Timing

Sometimes after we determine what God's plan is, we jump too quickly to try to accomplish what God said to do. We must learn to wait until the Lord directs us to take action.

For example, what would have happened if the Israelites had walked around Jericho for five days, and on the sixth day Joshua had said, "This plan is moving too slowly. Let's do it a different way.

"Let's walk around this city seven times *today* instead of tomorrow. That way we can blow the trumpets today and shout."

Do you know what would have happened to the walls of Jericho if Joshua had followed his own plan? Absolutely *nothing*!

If Joshua had gotten disgruntled and impatient and figured out his own plan, the Israelites would have lost the battle against Jericho. Joshua had to do it God's way to experience God's victory — and so do we!

The same is true with Gideon. If Gideon had tried to go to battle against the enemy with a fighting force of 22,000 or even 10,000 men, he would have been out of God's timing and ahead of God's plan. The Israelites would have faced overwhelming defeat simply because they didn't do it God's way. God's *way* brings God's *victory*!

You need to make sure you don't get ahead of God's plan too. It doesn't matter how many doors open for you in the natural, you must wait upon the Lord for *His* direction and *His* timing.

It doesn't matter how many people tell you, "You should do this," or "You should do that," wait before God in prayer until you receive *His* instructions. Who is in charge of your life, anyway? The Lord or other people?

So learn to wait before God in prayer. Continue to listen to what God is saying to you through His Word and by His Holy Spirit. Execute God's plan in God's timing.

If you will wait on God, even though the devil tries to hinder you, you can claim the victory that belongs to *God's* victory plan.

As you wait before God in prayer and listen for His direction, remember that you walk in God's victory plan by *faith*, not by how you *feel*. For instance, you might say, "But I don't feel like a victor. I don't have a job. I am behind in all my bills. I feel weak and insignificant."

No matter how you *feel*, the Word says you *are* on the victory side because you are in Christ (Rom. 8:37). Regardless of how you *feel*, God will make a way where there seems to be no way. But you'll have to follow God's plan completely before you can experience *His* victory. Wait before God in prayer until you know His timing.

Praise Defeats the Enemy's Strategy

Frequently in the Word of God when people just did exactly what God told them to do, the enemy turned and ran. Many times the people of God didn't even have to fight. God routed the enemy for them.

For example, praise is the battle strategy God used
to bring about His victory plan in fighting the
Ammonites. God instructed King Jehoshaphat to send
the praisers out in front, singing praises to God.

2 CHRONICLES 20:20-25
**20 And they rose early in the morning, and went
forth into the wilderness of Tekoa: and as they
went forth, Jehoshaphat stood and said, Hear me,
O Judah, and ye inhabitants of Jerusalem; Believe
in the Lord your God, so shall ye be established;
believe his prophets, so shall ye prosper.
21 And when he had consulted with the people, he
appointed singers unto the Lord, and that should
praise the beauty of holiness, as they went out
before the army, and to say, Praise the Lord; for
his mercy endureth for ever.
22 And when they began to sing and to praise, the
Lord set ambushments against the children of
Ammon, Moab, and mount Seir, which were come
against Judah; and they were smitten.
23 For the children of Ammon and Moab stood up
against the inhabitants of mount Seir, utterly to
slay and destroy them: and when they had made
an end of the inhabitants of Seir, every one helped
to destroy another.
24 And when Judah came toward the watch tower
in the wilderness, they looked unto the multitude,
and, behold, they were dead bodies fallen to the
earth, and none escaped.
25 And when Jehoshaphat and his people came to
take away the spoil of them, they found among
them in abundance both riches with the dead bodies, and precious jewels, which they stripped off
for themselves, more than they could carry away:
and they were three days in gathering of the spoil,
it was so much.**

God's victory plan in this case was for the Israelites to go out against the enemy singing praises. That doesn't make any sense in the natural, does it? But the Lord knew what would bring the victory.

The Israelites didn't even have to fight in this battle! They never lifted a finger. Verse 23 says that the enemy fought against themselves: ". . . *every one helped to destroy another.*"

By the time the Israelites got to the battlefield, it was all over. The dead bodies of the enemy lay all over the battlefield. The only thing the Israelites had to do to win this battle was to obey God.

God said, "March down the road singing, 'Praise the Lord; for His mercy endureth forever'" (2 Chron. 20:21). And the Israelites did it!

Some of you just need to start singing praises to God. For some of you, *your victory is waiting on your praise!* Start praising and start marching. If you'll do that, God will take care of your problem! Your problem isn't bigger than God. But part of your problem is that you're too concerned about the enemy.

In the old days in some Pentecostal circles, some folks used to stand up and testify, saying, "The devil's been after me all the day. Pray for me that I'll hold out till the end!"

Bless God! There's no such thing as holding out to the end. We should say, "Pray for me that I'll march on in God's victory plan and win victory after victory!"

You also hear people say, "Just pray that we can hold the fort!" But who's interested in just holding the fort? Let's go forward in the Lord's plan and take what belongs to us. That's the problem with some people. They're just barely holding on instead of possessing every single promise of God that belongs to them!

Friends, let's not just *hold on*. Let's take what God said belongs to us! Let's possess our inheritance in Christ! Let us live our lives fully to God's glory so He receives all the credit and praise.

But to walk in God's victory plan for your life, you'll have to listen to the Word. You will never know the *will* of God for your life until you know the *Word* of God.

What is the will of God for your life? In general, it's His will that you be filled with the Holy Spirit. It's His will to heal you. It's His will to provide for your needs. It's His will that you're a blessing to others.

Then God also has specific plans just for *your* life. And He will reveal those plans to you as you seek Him in prayer and in the Word.

Gideon had to know the specific will of God for his life. The angel of the Lord appeared to Gideon and said specifically just to him, ". . . *thou shalt save Israel from the hand of the Midianites: have not I sent thee?*" (Judges 6:14).

But Gideon wanted to know exactly what the Lord wanted him to do, and he wanted God to confirm that He had really spoken to him. That's why Gideon put out a fleece before the Lord (Judges 6:37). We don't need fleeces today, because we've got the Holy Spirit abiding in us to lead and guide us.

But remember, when the angel of the Lord talked to Gideon about God's plan, Gideon had no inner witness of the Holy Spirit to lead and guide him. He had to work with this supernatural manifestation totally in the natural realm because he wasn't born again.

Therefore, Gideon couldn't be led supernaturally by his spirit because his spirit wasn't alive unto God. The Israelites couldn't be led by their spirits. No one could until the new birth became available under the New Covenant (John 3:5-8).

We can be led by God the Holy Spirit in our own spirit (Rom. 8:14). The Bible says, *"Know ye not that ye are the temple of God, and that the Spirit of God dwelleth in you?"* (1 Cor. 3:16).

The Holy Ghost resides inside of you, in your spirit. You don't need fleeces. You just need to look to the Holy Spirit on the inside to give you His direction.

We also have the written Word of God to lead and guide us. That's why we should never try to go back under the Old Testament and put out a fleece like Gideon did.

But because Gideon was totally operating in the natural realm, he didn't know for sure that this was really God speaking to him.

After Gideon determined what God's plan was, he then had to determine God's timing.

For example, if Gideon had immediately taken his entire fighting force and rushed out to battle, he would have gotten things in a mess. He would have gotten ahead of God.

The same thing is true for us. We can know *what* God wants us to do, but then we need to wait before Him in prayer to know *when* He wants us to do it. Sometimes we jump too quickly.

Even when we know what God's plan is, sometimes we jump and run when we should be waiting before God in prayer for further instructions.

For example, Jehoshaphat received God's instructions. He knew exactly what God was telling him to do. God told him to put the singers out front and have them praise God as they marched along.

But notice that after King Jehoshaphat received his orders from the Lord, he waited until the next morning before going out to battle. Why did he do that? Because the Lord instructed the Israelites to go out the *next* morning.

2 CHRONICLES 20:13-18
13 And all Judah stood before the Lord, with their little ones, their wives, and their children.
14 Then upon Jahaziel . . . came the Spirit of the Lord in the midst of the congregation;
15 And he said, Hearken ye, all Judah, and ye inhabitants of Jerusalem, and thou king Jehoshaphat, Thus saith the Lord unto you, Be not afraid nor dismayed by reason of this great multitude; for the battle is not yours, but God's.
16 TOMORROW GO YE DOWN AGAINST THEM: behold, they come up by the cliff of Ziz; and ye shall find them at the end of the brook, before the wilderness of Jeruel.
17 Ye shall not need to fight in this battle: set yourselves, stand ye still, and see the salvation of the Lord with you, O Judah and Jerusalem: fear

not, nor be dismayed; tomorrow go out against them: for the Lord will be with you.
18 And Jehoshaphat bowed his head with his face to the ground: and all Judah and the inhabitants of Jerusalem fell before the Lord, worshipping the Lord.

Although the Israelites received God's instructions the afternoon before, they followed God's plan exactly by waiting until the next morning before executing it. If Jehoshaphat hadn't followed God's victory plan exactly as the Spirit of the Lord had instructed him by waiting until the next day to go to battle, the enemy probably wouldn't have been in the right location!

It's important to know God's timing so you don't get ahead of God. When you try to follow God's plan out of His time, His provision isn't there.

In First Kings 19:9-12, the prophet Elijah also learned the importance of waiting on God's timing.

God sent Elijah to the mountaintop to seek Him. Then came a mighty wind, an earthquake, and a fire — which were all supernatural occurrences. But God just used the wind, the fire, and the earthquake to get Elijah's attention. God didn't speak to Elijah through any of those things.

1 KINGS 19:9-12
9 And he [Elijah] came thither unto a cave, and lodged there; and, behold, the word of the Lord came to him, and he said unto him, What doest thou here, Elijah?
10 And he said, I have been very jealous for the Lord God of hosts: for the children of Israel have

forsaken thy covenant, thrown down thine altars,
and slain thy prophets with the sword; and I, even
I only, am left; and they seek my life, to take it
away.
11 And he said, Go forth, and stand upon the
mount before the Lord. And, behold, the Lord
passed by, and a great and strong WIND rent the
mountains, and brake in pieces the rocks before
the Lord; BUT THE LORD WAS NOT IN THE
WIND: and after the wind an EARTHQUAKE; BUT
THE LORD WAS NOT IN THE EARTHQUAKE:
12 And after the earthquake a FIRE; BUT THE
LORD WAS NOT IN THE FIRE: and after the fire A
STILL SMALL VOICE.

You see, the Lord used the wind, the fire, and the
earthquake to get Elijah's attention to let him know He
was going to speak to him. Elijah could have jumped
and run out to try to do God's will when he first heard
the wind.

Then when the earthquake and the fire came, he
could have thought, *This must be God!* and run out to
try to do God's will. But he didn't even know what God
wanted him to do yet. Notice, it was only with the still
small voice that God spoke and gave Elijah His instructions.

1 KINGS 19:15,16
15 And the Lord said unto him [Elijah], Go, return
on thy way to the wilderness of Damascus: and
when thou comest, anoint Hazael to be king over
Syria:
16 And Jehu the son of Nimshi shalt thou anoint
to be king over Israel: and Elisha the son of
Shaphat of Abel-meholah shalt thou anoint to be
prophet in thy room.

Many people jump and run when they hear the wind of the Holy Spirit blowing. They know God is moving and they get excited about it, but they just don't take time to hear what He's saying to *them*.

People might hear that the wind of the Holy Spirit is moving over in a certain church. So they jump and leave their home church to run over to that church. Then they hear that the wind of the Holy Spirit is blowing somewhere else, so they jump and run over there.

When the fire of the Holy Spirit falls somewhere else, they jump and run to another place. All the while, God is trying to speak to them by His still small voice on the inside of them, but they're so busy running here and there, they can't hear what He's saying!

They miss the real move of God in their own lives because God was trying to get something across to them by His Spirit, but they were too busy running around to hear Him!

Elijah had the sense to just sit still because the Lord wasn't in the wind, the fire, or the earthquake. God wanted to talk to Elijah by His *Spirit* — the still small voice.

We've got to learn to wait! Wait until the Lord is in it before we move. We can jump and run when the Lord is first trying to get our attention, but at that point, we probably won't even know what's He's really saying to us.

It doesn't matter how many doors open up for you or how many people try to tell you, "You've got to do this" or "You've got to do that." Who is in control of your life? *God* or other people?

You should stay put and wait until you know that God is speaking to you. When God is in it, His provision will be there for you. You'll be able to move out and obey Him because He'll make the way.

I'm not saying the devil won't try to hinder you. But you'll be able to move out in faith and obedience because God will abundantly make a way for you.

Elijah waited until he heard the still small voice, and the Lord was in it. He didn't have to wonder if God had spoken to him — when God spoke by His still small voice, Elijah *knew* God had spoken!

Too many Christians move out to do God's will every time there's a big flash — a supernatural move of God. They want to run here, there, and everywhere. But maybe they're not supposed to run every time they hear that God is on the move somewhere. Maybe they're supposed to stay put and find out what the Lord is saying to *them!*

The secret to following God's victory plan is this: Stay where the Lord wants you to stay! And do what the Lord wants *you* to do! Stay put until you know what God's plan is for you. Then be sure you know His timing.

It may not be God's timing for you to move into the next part of His plan for you just yet. For example, God may never have some people move from their home church. Others may move on to another local church. But no matter what — following God's plan brings victory and success.

You hear people say, "Yes, but *I* have all these plans. I told some people that I was going to do this. And I promised other people that I would do that."

That's the problem! You said what *you* were going to do — not what *God* was going to do through you. On the other hand, don't let the words of your mouth in times past put you under condemnation. Just do what you know God wants you to do now.

Sometimes when students graduate from RHEMA Bible Training Center, God tells them to stay put. Some of their friends come back into town and say, "Why are you still here? Why haven't you left yet?"

"Because God didn't tell me to go yet," they answer.

Some of those people who come back into town have been to fifteen different places and haven't made a success at any of them! God told them to wait, but they left out of God's timing, and they want to condemn others for not leaving town too.

But remember what brought Joshua success in God. He had to wait for God's timing before he could execute God's plan. He couldn't just run out after marching around Jericho five times and announce, "Hey! This is too slow! I've had it! We're going around seven times today. Then we're going to blow the trumpet, and maybe those walls will fall down."

If he'd done that, nothing would have happened. Sometimes it seems like believers want things to happen right now! Sometimes we pastors want things to happen quickly too. But we've got to do it God's way in God's time.

Joshua and the Israelites had to march for seven days. He could not get discouraged, disgruntled, dissatisfied, or try to hurry things up. He had to execute God's plan in God's way. And so do we!

God's Victory Plan in the New Testament

The Lord will always come through with His victory plan if we will just believe His Word. In the New Testament, God tells us very clearly His victory plan.

MARK 9:23
23 Jesus said unto him, IF THOU CANST BELIEVE, ALL THINGS ARE POSSIBLE TO HIM THAT BELIEVETH.

God's victory plan is based on believing. Believing what? Believing what God said in His Word and acting on it.

No matter what circumstance you face, just hold on to God's Word because help is on the way!

1 CORINTHIANS 10:13
13 There hath no temptation taken you but such as is common to man: but God is faithful, who will not suffer you to be tempted above that ye are able; but will with the temptation also make a way to escape, that ye may be able to bear it.

Sometimes people say, "Man, I'm in the midst of a storm." Even if you are, know that God is faithful. He won't allow you to be tempted more than you can bear. He promised He would make a way of escape for you.

1 CORINTHIANS 1:9
**9 GOD IS FAITHFUL, by whom ye were called
unto the fellowship of his Son Jesus Christ our
Lord.**

God is faithful. The Bible says, "Great is His faithfulness" (Lam. 3:23). So we can be sure that God will faithfully bring His victory plan to pass in our lives as we obey Him.

In the New Testament, Jesus tells us some more about His victory plan. He promised that He and His Father would make their abode in us.

JOHN 14:23
**23 Jesus answered and said unto him, If a man
love me, he will keep my words: and my Father
will love him, and WE WILL COME UNTO HIM,
AND MAKE OUR ABODE WITH HIM.**

Jesus also promised that He would never leave us or forsake us. God is on our side, and He's always waiting to be our Helper. The trouble with many Christians is that they don't ask God to help them. They try to make a success of His victory plan on their own, and it can't be done in human strength.

HEBREWS 13:5,6
**5 . . . for he [God] hath said, I will never leave
thee, nor forsake thee.**
**6 So that we may boldly say, THE LORD IS MY
HELPER, and I will not fear what man shall do
unto me.**

God promised to help us in the time of trouble. And with God on the inside of us, we have a Helper greater than any problem we could ever face. The Bible says, *"Ye are of God, little children, and have overcome them: because greater is he that is in you, than he that is in the world"* (1 John 4:4).

The Holy Spirit, the Greater One who lives in us, is greater than any problem the devil can throw our way! Besides that, God promised that no weapon that is formed against us shall prosper (Isa. 54:17).

You see, the victory has already been won by Jesus. Remember, the Bible says that you're not going to have to fight in this battle (2 Chron. 20:17). You don't have to fight the devil because Jesus already defeated him at Calvary's Cross. You just have to stand your ground on the Word and see the mercy and the delivering power of the Lord! Talk victory by talking the Word!

Some Christians seem to prefer taking off their coats, rolling up their sleeves, and getting in a fight. But the arm of flesh is not going to win you anything. On the other hand, the power of God will deliver you every time. God's power is contained in His Word, and the Word will triumph over the devil and every evil circumstance! Let the Word fight your battles for you!

Sometimes people say, "But I just don't *feel* like a victor."

It doesn't make any difference what you *feel*. You're still on the victory side if you're in Christ. It doesn't matter how you feel. It only matters what the Word promises. And God said He will make a way so you can walk in His victory plan.

1 CORINTHIANS 15:57
57 But thanks be to God, which GIVETH US THE VICTORY THROUGH OUR LORD JESUS CHRIST.

God will set you free. God will deliver you — if you'll just do things His way.

2 CORINTHIANS 2:14
14 Now thanks be unto God, which ALWAYS CAUSETH US TO TRIUMPH IN CHRIST, and maketh manifest the savour of his knowledge by us in every place.

It doesn't make any difference where you are now. No, you don't have to run over here or over there to receive the delivering power of God. This verse says that God will *always* cause you to triumph. Where? In every place, no matter where you are — just as long as you're in Christ!

Friend, don't let the devil steal your joy. Don't let the devil take away from you what belongs to you. The devil didn't give you your inheritance in Christ, and the devil can't take it away from you either — unless you let him.

COLOSSIANS 3:24
24 Knowing that of the Lord ye shall receive the reward of the inheritance: for ye serve the Lord Christ.

People may not understand your shouting when it's dark and bleak all around you — when there's not even a speck or ray of hope anywhere. But it doesn't matter whether or not they understand your faith in God.

The Bible says, "Thanks be to God who *always* causes us to triumph." The Greater One living inside of you will put you over in every circumstance if you'll just look to Him. He'll show you His victory plan in every dark circumstance and make a way for you to escape the devil's plans.

Get on the victory side with God! Then catch yourself if you start grumbling and complaining. Grab yourself by the collar and say, "What am I doing, giving place to the devil with my words! The Bible said, *'Neither give place to the devil'* [Eph. 4:27]. God, please forgive me. I purpose to only speak Your words of victory!"

People can talk about what the devil is doing in their lives. But I don't care what the devil is doing. It doesn't interest me in the least. What interests me is what Jesus Christ is doing on this earth — and what Jesus wants to do through me!

Jesus Christ came. He died on the Cross. He arose victorious. He sits at the right hand of the Father on High, making intercession for us. Thanks be to God, we are victors through Christ Jesus!

God has a plan for you! Follow His plan exactly, and it will always bring you *victory*! Remember, God does not intend for His plan to fail!

But you will have to get your eyes off your problem and look only to Jesus (Heb. 12:2). Listen to what God is saying to you. Then do God's will and follow *His* plan exactly.

If you obediently follow God as He shows you His victory plan, know beyond a shadow of a doubt that God *will* cause His plan to succeed. You will walk in the victory that is yours in Christ.

Chapter 3
Faith Expects the Best!

In order to walk in God's victory plan for your life, you're going to have to expect the best! You can't wallow around in doubt and unbelief, expecting the worst for your life and then go on and win great battles in God.

But it seems that human nature expects the worst. And even in the Word of God, there were people who expected the worst.

For example, David was a man of great faith. But we can see at least one time in his life when David experienced a lapse in his faith. He had been trusting God to deliver him from Saul, but at one point he got discouraged because Saul had been chasing him for so long, trying to kill him.

Finally, David got so discouraged, he started confessing negative things over his life. And what's worse, he believed them in his heart!

> **1 SAMUEL 27:1**
> 1 And David said in his heart, I SHALL NOW PERISH ONE DAY BY THE HAND OF SAUL....

If you've studied the story of Saul and David, you remember that Saul got jealous of David, and for many years, Saul sought to kill David. After being on the run from Saul for so long, David finally hit a low point in his faith and started anticipating the worst.

Let's look at what had happened just before David spoke these words here in First Samuel 27:1. Saul had never been able to catch up to David to kill him. But twice David crept unnoticed into Saul's camp. Both times David could have taken Saul's life, but he didn't.

The first time David spared Saul's life, Saul had gone into a cave in the wilderness of En-Gedi. David crept into the cave and cut off the skirt of Saul's robe without Saul's knowing it (1 Sam. 24:1-22). David could have killed Saul, but instead he spared Saul's life.

1 SAMUEL 24:1-12
1 And it came to pass, when Saul was returned from following the Philistines, that it was told him, saying, Behold, David is in the wilderness of En-gedi.
2 Then Saul took three thousand chosen men out of all Israel, and went to seek David and his men upon the rocks of the wild goats.
3 And he came to the sheepcotes by the way, where was a cave; and Saul went in to cover his feet: and David and his men remained in the sides of the cave.
4 And the men of David said unto him, Behold the day of which the LORD said unto thee, Behold, I will deliver thine enemy into thine hand, that thou mayest do to him as it shall seem good unto thee. Then David arose, and cut off the skirt of Saul's robe privily.
5 And it came to pass afterward, that David's heart smote him, because he had cut off Saul's skirt.

6   And he said unto his men, The Lord forbid that
I should do this thing unto my master, the Lord's
anointed, to stretch forth mine hand against him,
seeing he is the anointed of the Lord.
7   So David stayed his servants with these words,
and suffered them not to rise against Saul. But
Saul rose up out of the cave, and went on his way.
8   David also arose afterward, and went out of
the cave, and cried after Saul, saying, My lord the
king. And when Saul looked behind him, David
stooped with his face to the earth, and bowed
himself.
9   And David said to Saul, Wherefore hearest
thou men's words, saying, Behold, David seeketh
thy hurt?
10 Behold, this day thine eyes have seen how that
the Lord had delivered thee to day into mine hand
in the cave: and some bade me kill thee: but mine
eye spared thee; and I said, I will not put forth
mine hand against my lord; for he is the Lord's
anointed.
11 Moreover, my father, see, yea, see the skirt of
thy robe in my hand: for in that I cut off the skirt
of thy robe, and killed thee not, know thou and see
that there is neither evil nor transgression in mine
hand, and I have not sinned against thee; yet thou
huntest my soul to take it.
12 The Lord judge between me and thee, and the
Lord avenge me of thee: but mine hand shall not
be upon thee.

Even though it had been prophesied years before
that David would be king and rule over Israel (1 Sam.
16:1,12,13), for a long time it didn't look like that was
ever going to come to pass.

Can you imagine how weary David got just trying to
stay alive! No wonder at times the hope of becoming

king looked so impossible to him. It would have been so easy for him just to kill Saul and try to make the word of the Lord come true in his own strength.

The second time Saul tried to kill David, Saul took three thousand of his fighting men with him.

> **1 SAMUEL 26:2,7-13,18,21**
> **2** Then Saul arose, and went down to the wilderness of Ziph, having three thousand chosen men of Israel with him, to seek David in the wilderness of Ziph....
> **7** So David and Abishai came to the people by night: and, behold, Saul lay sleeping within the trench, and his spear stuck in the ground at his bolster: but Abner and the people lay round about him.
> **8** Then said Abishai to David, God hath delivered thine enemy into thine hand this day: now therefore let me smite him, I pray thee, with the spear even to the earth at once, and I will not smite him the second time.
> **9** And David said to Abishai, Destroy him not: for who can stretch forth his hand against the Lord's anointed, and be guiltless?
> **10** David said furthermore, As the Lord liveth, the Lord shall smite him; or his day shall come to die; or he shall descend into battle, and perish.
> **11** The Lord forbid that I should stretch forth mine hand against the Lord's anointed: but, I pray thee, take thou now the spear that is at his bolster, and the cruse of water, and let us go.
> **12** So David took the spear and the cruse of water from Saul's bolster; and they gat them away, and no man saw it, nor knew it, neither awaked: for they were all asleep; because a deep sleep from the Lord was fallen upon them.

13 Then David went over to the other side, and stood on the top of an hill afar off; a great space being between them. . . .
18 And he said, Wherefore doth my lord thus pursue after his servant? for what have I done? or what evil is in mine hand? . . .
21 Then said Saul, I have sinned: return, my son David: for I will no more do thee harm, because my soul was precious in thine eyes this day: behold, I have played the fool, and have erred exceedingly.

It was after these attempts on David's life that he began to despair and expect the worst even though the Lord had promised that he would be king over Israel.

Until this time, David had been trusting God to deliver him from Saul. But right after this incident with Saul, it seemed as though David just gave up. He should have known that God had a victory plan. But, instead, David suffered a lapse of faith.

It was then that David said, "I shall now perish one day by the hand of Saul." So David arose and went into Philistia and lived with the Philistines for a while. You see, because David expected the worst, he even went to live in the land of the enemy.

We can't blame David for fainting in faith when sometimes we've done the same thing. So many times when we're going through a hard time, we begin to expect the worst just like David did.

That reminds me of a story I read that shows that human nature sometimes expects the worst. A fellow was going to visit a certain pastor, but it was snowing out and the streets were icy. He had to walk to the pastor's house, and because the sidewalks were slick and treacherous, it was hard for him to keep from falling.

As he walked along, he remembered that this pastor's house was at the bottom of a steep incline. He began to think to himself, *I'll never be able to get down that hill to his house. I'll slide or I'll fall, and I'm going to hurt myself for sure!*

He almost decided to turn around and go home because he expected the worst. But he'd told this pastor that he would drop by, so he continued on, all the while expecting to find the worst possible situation when he got there.

But when he finally arrived, he found that the people had spread sand all over the hill. He had no problem whatsoever making his way down to the house!

What's *Your* Expectation?

I use that little story as an example to show you that so often, we're like that too. We expect the worst, so we almost turn back in our faith. Doubt always expects the worst; faith expects the best because it trusts in God.

Sometimes we allow ourselves to be tormented by thinking about what *could* happen. And so many times, the worst that we expect never actually materializes.

This is exactly where David was in his faith. Tormented by thoughts that Saul would eventually kill

him, he anticipated the worst. He thought he'd finally
die by Saul's hand.

But did David forget about God? Did he forget that
God had promised that *he* would rule over Israel? It
seems at this one weak moment in his life, David forgot
about God's victory plan for his life.

Just for a moment, David also lost sight of the protecting power of God. He lost his grip on the fact that
God had protected him every single time in the past
when Saul had tried to kill him.

For example, one time Saul stood right in the same
room with David and threw his spear at David, but he
couldn't hit him (1 Sam. 19:10). Saul was a good marks-
man, so it wasn't because of his poor aim that David's
life was spared.

God was taking care of David. God had a plan for
David's life, and He wasn't about to let the enemy kill
him. God had shown David His delivering power time
after time. In fact, David is the one who penned these
words in the Psalms because he'd experienced God's
delivering power so many times in his life.

PSALM 103:1-4
**1   Bless the Lord, O my soul: and all that is within
me, bless his holy name.**
**2   Bless the Lord, O my soul, and forget not all his
benefits:**
**3 Who forgiveth all thine iniquities; who healeth
all thy diseases;**
**4   WHO REDEEMETH THY LIFE FROM
DESTRUCTION; who crowneth thee with loving-
kindness and tender mercies.**

David knew the delivering power of God. But just for a moment, David forgot that God always plans for victory, so he fled in fear.

However, later David recovered his faith in God and held fast to it. He went on to become the King of Judah and then later the King of Israel. And in all the years that David walked with God, he pleased God. How do I know that? Because look what Paul said about David in the New Testament.

> **ACTS 13:22**
> **22 . . . he** [God] **raised up unto them David to be their king; to whom also he gave testimony, and said, I have found David the son of Jesse, A MAN AFTER MINE OWN HEART, which shall fulfil all my will.**

You see, David didn't stay in fear and defeat! He didn't keep on expecting the worst. He went on to enter into God's victory plan for his life. He accomplished everything God gave him to do.

How many times have we fainted in faith and fled in fear? That hinders the plan of God from being fulfilled in our lives. But we've probably all been tempted to flee from negative circumstances some time in our lives.

When we focus our eyes on the difficult circumstances instead of trusting in God, fear shuts down faith! When we focus our attention on the problem instead of on God, it's easy to lose sight of the power of God to deliver us.

It's when we let our shield of faith down that our faith is weakened. Weak faith opens the door to despair. By focusing on the problem, we can forget that God promised us the victory in every circumstance!

Often we allow ourselves to be tormented by thinking about all the bad things that *could* happen to us. But, in reality, most of the bad things we think about never actually happen.

We should know that God has already provided a victory plan for us — a way of escape out of every difficulty! All God's promises are yea and amen in Christ! It's up to us in faith to just walk out the victory that God already promised us in Christ.

So even though we've all failed in our faith from time to time, we can still go on to victory! We, too, can accomplish everything that God has for us.

Daniel's Lions' Den

Let's look at someone else in the Bible who was surrounded by evil circumstances. If he succeeded to walk in God's victory plan for his life despite great opposition, so can we!

The great prophet Daniel had been taken into captivity by the Babylonians as a young man. But even in captivity in a heathen nation, Daniel went to his window every day and prayed to God.

Daniel's enemies had tricked the Babylonian king, Darius, into signing a decree that said, "Whoever prays to any god except the king will be thrown to the lions."

DANIEL 6:5-10

5　Then said these men, We shall not find any occasion against this Daniel, except we find it against him concerning the law of his God.

6　Then these presidents and princes assembled together to the king, and said thus unto him, King Darius, live for ever.

7　All the presidents of the kingdom, the governors, and the princes, the counsellors, and the captains, have consulted together to establish a royal statute, and to make a firm decree, that whosoever shall ask a petition of any God or man for thirty days, save of thee, O king, he shall be cast into the den of lions.

8　Now, O king, establish the decree, and sign the writing, that it be not changed, according to the law of the Medes and Persians, which altereth not.

9　Wherefore king Darius signed the writing and the decree.

10　Now when Daniel knew that the writing was signed, he went into his house; and his windows being open in his chamber toward Jerusalem, he KNEELED UPON HIS KNEES THREE TIMES A DAY, and PRAYED, and GAVE THANKS BEFORE HIS GOD, as he did aforetime.

When Daniel's enemies caught him praying, they went to the king and said, "All right, King. What happens to the man that defies this decree?"

Darius answered, "He'll be cast into the lions' den."

These evil men said, "Well, this Daniel you like so much hasn't paid any attention to your decree. He's still praying three times a day to his God." Then the king realized he'd made a mistake. Daniel had found favor with him, and the king didn't want Daniel to die. But once the king had decreed a law, there was nothing he could do to change it — so Daniel was thrown to the lions.

> **DANIEL 6:16,17**
> **16 Then the king commanded, and they brought Daniel, and CAST HIM INTO THE DEN OF LIONS. Now the king spake and said unto Daniel, Thy God whom thou servest continually, he will deliver thee.**
> **17 And a stone was brought, and laid upon the mouth of the den; and the king sealed it with his own signet, and with the signet of his lords; that the purpose might not be changed concerning Daniel.**

But look at the difference between Darius' fearful reaction and Daniel's trust in God in this hopeless situation.

> **DANIEL 6:18**
> **18 Then the king went to his palace, and passed the night fasting: neither were instruments of music brought before him: and his sleep went from him.**

Darius had a restless night. He anticipated the worst because he didn't know God. He couldn't sleep because he was worried about Daniel. While Darius stayed up all night worrying about Daniel, Daniel slept fine! With the first light of morning, King Darius ran down to the lions' den, and cried, "Daniel! Was your God able to save you?"

Daniel answered, "Never fear, O King! I'm here, and everything is fine. My God has taken care of me."

DANIEL 6:19-23

19 Then the king arose very early in the morning, and went in haste unto the den of lions.

20 And when he came to the den, he cried with a lamentable voice unto Daniel: and the king spake and said to Daniel, O Daniel, servant of the living God, is thy God, whom thou servest continually, able to deliver thee from the lions?

21 Then said Daniel unto the king, O king, live for ever.

22 My God hath sent his angel, and hath shut the lions' mouths, that they have not hurt me: forasmuch as before him innocency was found in me; and also before thee, O king, have I done no hurt.

23 Then was the king exceeding glad for him, and commanded that they should take Daniel up out of the den. So Daniel was taken up out of the den, and no manner of hurt was found upon him, because he believed in his God.

You see, Daniel knew the delivering power of God. He trusted in God's victory plan — even when he was thrown into a pack of hungry lions! He stayed calm and peaceful through the whole ordeal.

I can just imagine Daniel herding all those lions together in that den, so he could use one of them for a pillow and the rest of them to stay warm.

You see, faith *rests*, but unbelief wallows in restlessness and fear. In this case, Darius expected the worst. But Daniel lived by faith, so he expected the best because he knew that the enemy never catches God by surprise! God always plans for victory! Faith always expects the best.

Don't Faint in Your Faith!

What do these biblical accounts have to do with us today? Plenty! The devil is always trying to get believers to faint in their faith in God and think the worst about every situation.

Satan is always trying to get believers to think thoughts of doubt and unbelief, dread and fear. Stripped of their faith in God, the devil can get believers to think the worst. Then they begin to doubt God's victory plan for their lives.

Once they get into doubt, believers will never be able to walk in that supernatural realm of faith that brings God's victory on the scene — even though victory already belongs to them.

That's why you cannot afford to think negatively when you are believing God for something. If you've been standing strong in faith, but then waver and begin to get into doubt and fear, you can nullify your faith.

For instance, when you listen to the news reports about all the terrible problems in the world today, you can't afford to start meditating on all the negativity. You can't think negatively like the world thinks.

You've got to anticipate the best because you serve a God who has already planned for your victory and success! You need to confidently speak your faith by saying, "No matter what happens, God will take care of me."

When we hear bad news, it's easy to let our natural mind immediately begin to anticipate the worst. The world's pressures are continually bombarding our natural senses.

But if we really know how to believe God and we know the Word, we can't afford to allow outside pressures to bombard our ears, our eyes, and our minds.

Don't let the world's negativity affect you! Expect the best from God! Expect that what God said to you will come to pass.

Now I'm not saying that we're supposed to act silly and not plan for the future. We're supposed to exercise some common sense. But I'm talking about learning how to believe God so what God says outweighs the world's negativity.

For instance, God said He will supply our needs (Phil. 4:19). How will He do it? I don't know. It's not my responsibility to figure out *how* God will fulfill His own promises. It's not your problem either. That's God's business.

But since God made the universe, He's big enough to meet your needs. If He can fashion the world with one fling of His almightiness, I think He can solve your problems too!

Your responsibility is just to believe God! Consider His Word as the final authority — not natural circumstances or man's opinions. Remember what the Bible says: *"Behold, I am the Lord, the God of all flesh: is there any thing too hard for me?"* (Jer. 32:27).

Someone might ask, "Well, aren't *you* concerned about all the problems in the world? Aren't you concerned about things like inflation?"

Yes, I'm concerned about the problems in this world. But I'm not going to *worry* about them. There's a difference. Besides, if a person centers all his attention on what everyone says about the world's problems, he'll begin to anticipate the worst until he eventually sinks into despair.

I'd rather read God's Word and see what *God* says about the situation! God promised He'd take care of His people. He promised that He always has a plan for victory.

Someone once asked me what I was going to do about our rising cost of living.

I answered, "I'm going to do what the Bible says. The Bible says, 'Render unto Caesar what is Caesar's, and unto God what belongs to God' [Matt. 22:21]. So I'm going to render to the government what belongs to it, and I'm going to render to God what belongs to Him.

"Then I'm going to do what the Word of God says. The Word of God says that whatever I believe that's in line with the Word, I can receive!"

It doesn't help anyone to get in turmoil over what's going on in our world today. We need to constantly be aware that no matter what happens around us, God is still the same. He can take care of us because down through the ages, His plan for victory has never changed.

In fact, God and His Word are the only things in this universe that don't change. And God has a plan for victory for each one of our lives — no matter what happens in this world.

God promised that He would supply your needs. Maybe He's supplying your needs right now through

your paycheck. But your trust and security shouldn't be
in your job. Your security in life should be based on God
and His Word.

Remember that Jesus said, "Heaven and earth
shall pass away, but My Word will *never* pass away"
(Matt. 24:35).

What does that mean? That means that since God
promised us victory in every situation — then if we'll do
our part and believe Him — victory will be ours in
every circumstance! God said it. I believe it. And that
settles it!

In Mark 16, we see another biblical example of some
people who anticipated the worst. They weren't trusting
in their Heavenly Father's victory plan that He'd fashioned from the foundation of the world.

MARK 16:1-4
**1   And when the sabbath was past, Mary Magda-
lene, and Mary the mother of James, and Salome,
had bought sweet spices, that they might come
and anoint him.
2   And very early in the morning the first day of
the week, they came unto the sepulchre at the rising of the sun.
3   And they said among themselves, Who shall roll
us away the stone from the door of the sepulchre?
4   And when they looked, they saw that the stone
was rolled away: for it was very great.**

It was the first Easter morning, and the women
were on their way to Jesus' tomb. They were worried
because they couldn't figure out who was going to roll
away the stone in front of the tomb. They were expecting the worst.

They didn't realize that God knew exactly what was going on. He'd already planned the victory for His people through Jesus' death, burial, and resurrection.

However, the women were expecting the worst. They talked among themselves, saying, "It took strong men to roll that stone over the mouth of the tomb. Who's going to roll that stone away? We can't do it; we're just too weak."

But when the women got to the tomb, they found out they didn't need to roll the stone away at all! God had already taken care of it. It had been rolled away by angels!

Maybe you've got some stones and boulders of hindrance that are blocking your way. That's not too hard for God. It doesn't matter if God needs to use an angel to move those stones of hindrance out of your path! He can do it. Nothing is too hard for Him.

Worry Negates Faith

We need to realize that worrying about situations instead of trusting God just negates our faith. A lot of believers are worried about this, that, and the other thing. Some even spend hours in torment, worrying, *What's going to happen to me?*

But if you'll just follow God and cast your care on Him, you'll find out that when you get to the situation you're so worried about, God will have already taken care of it.

You just need to talk your problem over with God, stand on His promises, and then trust Him with it. Then like the women at the tomb, you'd discover that God has already taken care of the situation before you get there!

For instance, I once talked to someone who was worried because he had to appear before a magistrate about a particular legal matter. He told me, "I wonder what's going to be the outcome of all this?" He was worried and anticipating the worst.

I answered, "I want to tell you something. If you could have fixed this situation by yourself, you'd already have done it. Why don't you just lean on the Word of God and take it a step at a time?"

The man decided to take my advice. So he put God's Word to work in the situation. And when he finally appeared before the magistrate, he found out that all the worry and turmoil he'd gone through was for nothing. The entire situation had worked out fine.

Sometimes we do that too. We anticipate the worst about a situation and allow the enemy to play with our minds. That's why we need to put the Word first in our minds and hearts instead of the enemy's fear and torment.

Now I'm not telling you to act unwisely. If you need an attorney, get an attorney. But what I am telling you is this: If you know how to believe God and stand your ground on the Word — you'll find out that the Word is the final authority, even over negative circumstances.

What do I mean when I say the Word is the final authority over your problems? That means that your circumstances have to become subject to the Word. That's why you *can* expect the best in God.

When you stand your ground on God's Word, His Word changes natural circumstances!

I personally try to live by Luke 1:37: *"For with God nothing shall be impossible."* In fact, someone once said to me, "When you're trying to accomplish a goal, you don't know how to take no for an answer, do you?"

I answered, "No, I don't. I just believe that with God the statement 'It can't be done' does not apply to *any* situation."

It's not that I put faith in *my* natural ability. I just believe what the Word says: *"I can do all things through Christ which strengtheneth me"* (Phil. 4:13). Nothing is impossible with God, so if I'm hooked up with God, nothing is impossible!

I don't believe most Christians have really gotten hold of Philippians 4:13. They read it, but it hasn't registered on their hearts. That verse says we can do *all* things — not because of who *we* are, but because of *whose* we are! The Greater One within empowers us.

I believe that with God, there is always a way if we'll just develop strong faith in the Word of God. But you've got to be able to say, "I *can* do it — not in myself. But with Christ I *can* do whatever needs to be done because I'm in Him."

Some people relegate this verse of Scripture just to spiritual things. They think it's only *spiritual* things they can do because of Christ. But Paul wasn't talking just about spiritual things. No matter what needs to be done, I can do all things through Christ who strengthens me — even natural things. That means I can tap into Christ's strength and His wisdom about any situation. Think about that!

Some people say, "Wait a minute! You're going to pump people up so they get egotistical and conceited! It's conceited to say, '*I* can do all things!'"

But, you see, we're not saying we can do anything in our own strength. We're not the ones doing the work. Yes, we put our action and our faith into the task. But it's Christ who gives us the strength, the wisdom, and the power to accomplish what we need to do.

There is *nothing* we can't handle if we know how to abide in Christ. Then we don't get credit for the exploits we do for God — Jesus does!

JOHN 15:7
7 If ye abide in me, and my words abide in you, ye shall ask what ye will, and IT SHALL BE DONE UNTO YOU.

Have you grabbed hold of the reality of this verse? The problem with a lot of believers is that they don't know how to really *abide* in Christ. They're walking out of Christ, so to speak, by not resting in Him.

You've got to rely on God's Word to abide in Him. If you don't have His Word as an anchor, you'll expect the worst, instead of believing God for the best. That's not faith! Remember, faith is what pleases God (Heb. 11:6).

I remember one time I was in a certain country, and I went with several other people to the airport. The people at the airport told us, "Your bags are too heavy. You can't put them on the airplane."

Well, many people started unpacking their bags, giving away their clothing to the people who worked at the airport. But I needed everything that was in my bag because I was on my way to another foreign city to preach.

I said to the people I was traveling with, "Now wait a minute! Something isn't right about this! After all, I'm not on this trip for my health or as a tourist. I'm on this trip for the ministry."

I refused to accept the worst. I decided to put my faith out in this situation. So I just calmly said to myself, "They say this can't be done. But it can be done because Jesus said that we can do all things through Christ, and nothing is impossible to him who believes. I believe my baggage with everything in it can go on this trip!" That was my faith talking.

I just waited around there for a little while, and finally, I went back to the baggage counter. I said, "I need to check my bag."

The man at the desk said, "I told you awhile ago, you can't check this bag. It's too heavy."

So I waited a little while longer. I saw him leave, and another person came to the desk. I went up to the desk, and I said, "I need to check my bag."

He said, "Fine. Where are you going?"

I said, "Johannesburg."

"Oh, all right," he said, and he threw my baggage onto the airplane baggage rack!

You see, sometimes you just have to persevere in your faith and keep on believing God even when some people say, "It can't be done!" If you'll speak your faith, *God* will get involved in the situation.

You've got to stay in faith and expect the best. In fact, expecting the best is expecting God to act on your behalf. That's faith in action!

Just because you experienced a victory *yesterday* is no sign you're going to be ready to stand against the devil *tomorrow*. You won't be able to unless you keep yourself spiritually fit.

Sometimes you'll have to stand your ground even when the storms of life are raging all around you. I didn't say it would always be easy. You have to make a decision *every day* to stand in faith and proclaim, "God, I believe You! You promised me the victory in every circumstance, and I put You in remembrance of Your Word."

Faith Expects the Word To Triumph

Can you stand strong in faith on the Word when the storms of life are tossing you to and fro? Can you declare God's Word and expect the victory when circumstances are raging against you? Can you say, "I believe God! I am more than a conqueror through Christ who loves me"?

You need to develop confident expectation of victory in your life so you can live in God's victory plan for *you*. Faith always expects the best. But you'll have to abide in Christ before you can expect the best in every situation. That means you'll have to abide in His *Word*. Then you can expect the best because you're expecting victory to come from the Word — and God is always faithful to His Word!

You see, *faith in God causes you to anticipate victory.* Expect God to usher in His victory plan in your life! Begin to *talk the best* because you *expect the best*.

Don't talk about what you *don't* have. Talk about what you *do* have. Talk about who you are and what you possess in Christ. Talk about what is good and edifying so you can be built up, not torn down.

Don't be like David when he experienced a lapse of faith and began to doubt God and anticipate the worst. Claim what the Bible says: "I can do all things through Christ who strengthens me. God promised me that nothing is impossible with Him. God promised to take care of me, no matter what! So I don't care what happens, God's Word works!"

Somebody may say, "That's a very simple approach." Well, Jesus said that's the way to walk with God. He basically said to be as a little child in the simplicity of your faith (Mark 10:15).

For instance, when you promise a little child you'll give him a present, he believes you. He doesn't keep coming back to you, asking if it's really going to happen. He expects you to keep your promise. He simply expects the best!

Let's be the same way with God. Let's say, "God said it, and I expect Him to do it. I expect the answer — not because of who I am, but because of *whose* I am."

But you won't receive the answer you're believing for just by getting head knowledge of the Word. And you sure won't receive answered prayer by *wishing* your answer would come. You've got to exercise active faith.

You'll have to abide in the Word and feed your spirit on the truth of God's Word until you believe in your heart that you've received your answer. Then you've got to speak what you believe with your mouth.

You have to *expect* your answer to manifest in the natural, no matter what you feel, see, taste, touch, or smell. When you feed your faith on the Word, you strengthen your faith so God can perform wonders for you.

But I'll tell you what! You won't be able to feed your heart and mind on junk and do exploits for God. That's why it's up to you whether or not you ever walk in God's victory plan for your life. But if you'll keep your faith strong by basing it on the Word, nothing will be impossible to you through God.

God promised that He's going to take care of us. I don't care what happens in the world, God's Word works. If God could take care of unbelieving Israelites, wandering around in the wilderness for forty years, God can provide for us!

If inflation goes sky high and God needs to, He can still rain down manna from Heaven. We could simply go out on our front porch and collect manna, gather it up, and take it inside to feed our families.

If God could do that for His earthly children, the Israelites, He can do that for His spiritual children — you and I! I believe it's just that simple for God to take care of us. Why do I believe it's simple? Because my trust is in the Word of God.

I don't care what comes or what goes. I don't care who's in office, who's out of office, or whether we've even got an office. I don't care what party is ruling or not ruling, or whether there even is a ruling party!

In other words, it doesn't make any difference what's going on in this world, God will take care of us. God's victory plan — His Word — never fails.

So don't *ever* anticipate the worst again! Don't allow yourself to faint in your faith. Expect God to show you His victory plan for *your* life. Determine to develop *strong* faith in God and His Word so you can always walk in God's victory plan!

Chapter 4
Victory or Defeat?

Victory or defeat — it's your choice! Did you know that victory or defeat in life is up to you? Why? Because Jesus Christ already purchased your freedom in every area of life. Now it's up to you to walk in the victory that Jesus purchased for you.

> **EXODUS 14:13,14**
> 13 And Moses said unto the people, FEAR YE NOT, STAND STILL, AND SEE THE SALVATION OF THE LORD, which he will shew to you today: for the Egyptians whom ye have seen today, ye shall see them again no more for ever.
> 14 The Lord shall fight for you, and ye shall hold your peace.

In studying a particular passage of Scripture, we can gain a lot of valuable insight if we understand the setting in which certain things were spoken.

For example, when you first read the Scriptures above, you get the impression that Moses was speaking very calmly and quietly to the children of Israel. But if you look at the circumstances the Israelites were in, you find out that the situation was anything but a calm one!

71

Approximately two million Israelites (six hundred thousand men plus women and children) had just come out of Egypt in the midst of mass confusion. All the firstborn of the Egyptians had been slain by the last plague that came upon Egypt. The Egyptians gave away their most valuable possessions to the Israelites just to get them to leave so the plagues would stop (Exod. 3:22;12:35,36).

When Moses said, "Fear not, stand still, and see the salvation of the Lord," the Israelites were standing on the banks of the Red Sea. As they surveyed the vast Red Sea that stood before them, they realized to their horror that the ruthless Egyptian army was rapidly overtaking them from the rear.

There was no way of escape! There weren't any boats around to carry such a vast multitude with their livestock and belongings across the Red Sea. Only wilderness extended to the left and right of them. And they sure couldn't turn back! They were trapped!

EXODUS 14:9,10
9 But the Egyptians pursued after them, all the horses and chariots of Pharaoh, and his horsemen, and his army, and overtook them encamping by the sea, beside Pi-hahiroth, before Baal-zephon.
10 And when Pharaoh drew nigh, the children of Israel lifted up their eyes, and, behold, the Egyptians marched after them; and they were sore afraid: and the children of Israel cried out unto the Lord.

I imagine some of you have felt that same kind of hopelessness because of circumstances that seemed to

surround you and close in on you. Maybe you felt
trapped by circumstances that were beyond your control. Can you identify with these people who were faced
with such an impossible situation?

Every time the Israelites looked over their shoul-
ders, the enemy was getting a little closer. In fact, they
could hear the beating of the horses' hooves as the
Egyptians marched determinedly across the desert. The
Israelites could even see the dust swirling from the
Egyptians' chariot wheels.

As the Egyptians got closer and closer, the Israelites
could hear the voices of the soldiers rise to a mighty
crescendo out in that desert. And the Israelites could
probably tell from the tone of those voices as they urged
one another to catch the Israelite slaves, that the Egyptian army was in no mood to take captives. The Egyptians were probably prepared to kill every single
Israelite!

Facing such frightening circumstances, the children
of Israel turned against Moses.

EXODUS 14:10-12
**10 And when Pharaoh drew nigh, the children of
Israel lifted up their eyes, and, behold, the Egyptians marched after them; and they were sore
afraid: and the children of Israel cried out unto
the Lord.**
**11 And they said unto Moses, Because there were
no graves in Egypt, hast thou taken us away to die
in the wilderness? wherefore hast thou dealt thus
with us, to carry us forth out of Egypt?**
**12 Is not this the word that we did tell thee in
Egypt, saying, Let us alone, that we may serve the**

Egyptians? For it had been better for us to serve the Egyptians, than that we should die in the wilderness.

You see, these people were only looking at the physical circumstances. They were looking at the natural. Natural circumstances will always scream at you, "It's impossible! It can't be done! God won't deliver you this time." The Israelites forgot to look at the God of the impossible!

You know yourself that your feelings will always tell you, "It's not possible!" That's why you should never rely on your feelings to determine your faith. God's Word alone should determine your faith.

But Moses' outlook on impossible situations was different than the other Israelites. His attitude was different too. His eyes were not fixed on the circumstances that spelled only defeat.

Why was Moses' outlook entirely different? Because he had been in desperate situations before and God had delivered him. Moses had stood with his brother Aaron in Pharoah's court when Aaron threw his rod on the floor and it turned into a serpent.

Moses had also watched as the devil's crowd — Pharoah's magicians — duplicated this feat blow for blow and stride for stride. The magicians' rods turned into serpents too. That's a desperate situation! Here Moses was trying to perform mighty feats for God, and the devil starts matching him stride for stride. But that wasn't the end of the story.

Even in that desperate situation, Moses listened to God. He didn't get all upset and faint in his faith. He remembered God's Word to him. God had told Moses that He would do wonders in Pharoah's court *"That they may believe that the Lord God of their fathers, the God of Abraham, the God of Isaac, and the God of Jacob, hath appeared unto thee"* (Exodus 4:5).

So without fear or wavering, Moses just stood fast on God's word to him. And he and Aaron watched as their rod turned into a serpent and swallowed up the magicians' serpents. Then Moses reached out and grabbed that serpent by the tail, and it turned back into a rod (Exod. 7:8-12). Pharoah's magicians were confounded and put to shame!

So, you see, Moses had been in desperate situations before and had watched God work His mighty victory plan. Therefore, he knew his only hope was in God. Remember, Moses had not only talked with God at the burning bush, but he'd also watched as the bush was set ablaze with fire but never burned up (Exod. 3:2)!

Not only had Moses talked to God, but he had also been an eyewitness to the unlimited, omnipotent power of God that is available to those who will believe!

Yes, Moses had experienced the delivering hand of God in difficult situations. And he knew that when God has a victory plan, no matter what the devil's crowd tries to do, if he stayed obedient to God, he'd come out the victor. God never plans for failure.

So as Moses surveyed this desperate situation at the Red Sea, he didn't deny the physical obstacles that made the Israelites' escape impossible. He saw the Red Sea stretched out before them. He could hear the Egyptian army closing in on them.

But he also remembered the charge that the Lord had given him. God had told Moses, *"Come now therefore, and I will send thee unto Pharaoh, that thou mayest bring forth my people the children of Israel out of Egypt"* (Exod. 3:10).

God knew the Israelites would be confronted with the Red Sea. And God knew the Egyptians would pursue the Israelites (Exod. 14:4). Had God planned for failure? Of course not! God was just working His victory plan.

I'm sure Moses was overcome with thoughts of victory, not defeat. He may have thought: *I am responsible for these people. I know I've heard from God. Therefore, God has a plan. And God's plans only lead to victory!*

Some of you who are the heads of your families are facing similar circumstances right now in your lives. No, you're not literally trying to cross the Red Sea with Pharoah's army closing in behind you. But you are in desperate circumstances.

You've even said to yourself, *I know I heard from God! But look at all these negative circumstances! What am I going to do?* But let me ask you a question. Are you thinking thoughts of victory or thoughts of defeat?

Your Triumph Is in the Word

If you are going to enter fully into God's victory plan, you're going to have to stand your ground on

God's Word. The Word is the only thing that's going to turn your situation around. It's the only thing that can hold you up when circumstances seem to be closing in all around you.

You need to know that all the victory you will ever need in life is contained in the promises in God's Word.

In fact, because of God's promises to you in His Word, you can always triumph in Christ. But you'll have to feed your faith on the Word of God.

As you put the Word first before the circumstances, the Word will overcome those circumstances. You'll look around for the impossibilities, and you won't be able to find them!

I'm sure as Moses surveyed this impossible situation, he realized that natural means and natural power could not handle this situation. No one on earth could help the Israelites!

If only some of us would come to that realization! Many times we have the attitude that we can handle the job or the problem all by ourselves. But we can't. All we do is make a mess of it.

Our victory comes in relying on the Word. It's God's strength that will put us over in the situation! Why rely on our strength when we've got the strength of Almighty God behind us!

Moses knew that to get out of that situation, he would have to do what God had instructed him to do. What set Moses apart from the others was that he knew it wasn't *his* responsibility to make what God said come to pass. That was *God's* responsibility!

We need to learn that same lesson. Most of us find ourselves in trouble when we take the responsibility for making what God told us come to pass. But that's not our responsibility. God can make His own victory plan come to pass all by Himself. All we have to do is walk in obedience to God's victory plan.

Moses knew that. He knew that his responsibility was to lead the children of Israel, not to personally protect them and provide for them. That was an impossible job for just one man alone. That was *God's* responsibility. Only God could do that anyway.

All God told Moses to do was "Go! Lead My people out of the bondage of Egypt into the freedom of the Promised Land!"

All of us are walking on this road of life. We've probably all experienced our own "Egypt" that we've needed God to deliver us out of in life. And we all have our own "promised land" in life that's based on the promises in God's Word and our inheritance in Christ.

God wants us to each achieve His best in our lives. So when we hear God tell us to do something, it's our responsibility to do it. Then it's God's responsibility to make sure we're taken care of in any test or trial because we've been obedient to walk in His victory plan.

When you get hold of how to work with God so He can bring about His victory plan, you can lie down and go to sleep at night in the midst of all the turmoil and cares of life — and sleep like a baby!

But too many of us walk the floor in the middle of the night, wringing our hands, crying, "Oh, God! What am I going to do?" instead of lying down and sleeping in the sweetness of the Holy Spirit. We can sleep in perfect peace when our full trust is in God!

All your worrying and fretting won't help you anyway. In fact, it just makes things worse because it gets you out of faith! Besides, worrying and fretting do not give God anything to work with on your behalf because it's fear at work — not faith!

Actually, I'll tell you what your negative thoughts and confessions do. They give the devil fuel to attack you, because you're not speaking faith, and you're not putting your trust in God.

If you would ignore the devil's worry and start speaking the promises of God, you'd put Satan to flight! It's very hard for someone to pester you if you don't let the things he does bother you.

For example, if you had older brothers or sisters who continually pestered you when you were a kid, you know what I mean. When they found out that you wouldn't let them annoy you anymore, they'd quit!

That's how you need to get with Satan! If you would just learn to rest in the Holy Spirit when the devil tries to bring his worry to your mind, it would have a mighty discouraging effect on him! Who's interested in hanging around — just to be ignored!

Our problem many times is that we spend too much time talking about what the devil is doing. He just loves that! I don't want to waste my time talking about the devil's plans. I'd rather talk about Jesus Christ and His victory plan for my life. I'd rather talk about the power and authority God has over the devil!

When Moses was confronted with that impossibility at the Red Sea, he didn't waste his time talking about the enemy — about Pharoah's vast army approaching them. He realized that it was only God's power that could deliver them from Pharoah's army, so he focused only on God. He had learned a principle that was later to be recorded in the Bible: *". . . Not by might, nor by power, but by my spirit, saith the Lord of hosts"* (Zech. 4:6).

Think about Moses' plight for a moment. Just imagine how many ships and equipment you'd need to transport two million people across the Red Sea, plus their livestock and belongings. That's a lot of people!

It was in the midst of these desperate circumstances that Moses spoke the word of the Lord to the people. He said, *"Fear ye not, stand still, and see the salvation of the Lord, which he will shew to you today . . ."* (Exod. 14:13). That's faith!

In other words, even as the Egyptians were closing in on them, Moses began to preach faith in God to those unbelieving Israelites. Let me paraphrase what he might have said if he had been talking today's language.

He may have said something like this to the Israelites: "Hey, what's the matter with you people anyway? Don't you know the Lord God Jehovah is going to take care of us? Don't be afraid!

"Don't allow yourselves to get worried and con-
cerned about this circumstance! Forget it! Look to God.
Have you forgotten about God's supernatural power?
Who do you think got us out of Egypt in the first place?
Do you really think God brought us this far just to let
us die?

"Don't you know God is never taken by surprise? He
always has a plan to bring victory, not defeat! The word
'defeat' is not even in His vocabulary!

"God cares about you, so just stay in faith, and
watch Him work. God already has His victory plan all
figured out. Why cast away your confidence when God
Almighty is more than enough to deliver us!"

Moses challenged the Israelites, saying, "You just
stand still, and you will be awestruck at the mighty
power of God demonstrated to you and your children."

God is saying these same words to *you* today — no
matter what situation you may be facing: "Stand still
by standing in faith on the promises of God, and watch
God's salvation come to *you!*"

You may be facing a circumstance as impossible as
crossing the Red Sea. But if God could deliver the
Israelites, don't you think He can deliver you?

Your Focus Determines
Your Victory or Defeat

You see, because the Israelites continually spoke
negative words, they reduced their faith to *little* faith.
Their faith was overshadowed by the circumstances.

They allowed what they could see with their physical senses to overwhelm them.

Many of us have seen the power of God ministered on our behalf as we've walked down life's road. We've even seen God demonstrate His power on behalf of our friends and family members. Yet when we find ourselves in difficult circumstances, sometimes we let those negative circumstances overshadow our faith and rob us of our confidence in God.

Maybe you're not facing a problem right now. But let me tell you — difficulties come to all of us. I don't care what your name is or how many faith tapes you've got in your library; I don't care how many faith books you've read, or how many confessions you make — the enemy will still try to bring the problems of life against you.

But did you know that it's not the problems of life that defeat you? No, it's not, because God Himself promised to deliver you out of them all. The Bible says, *"Nay, in all these things we are MORE THAN CON-QUERORS through him that loved us"* (Rom. 8:37). Therefore, problems can't defeat you unless you *allow* them to defeat you.

If we're *more than* conquerors, that means with God's help we can *more than* succeed in this life. Actually, it's what we focus on in the midst of the trouble that determines our victory or defeat.

And if you don't guard against negativity, but you focus only on the problem, you can become full of fear, despair, and anxiety. It may even look like you're going to fail, but if you'll just stand on the promises of God, you can't fail because *God* can't fail. His *Word* can't fail, so if you're relying on His *Word*, *you* can't fail!

That's where the children of Israel made their mistake. Instead of remembering what God promised — that He would deliver them from the Egyptians — they became so engrossed in their circumstances that they could not see God.

We do that too. So many times, we get so engrossed in the tests and trials that we cannot see the victory God promised us. We lose sight of His promises to us.

The frustrations of life come to us all. They come to you; they come to me. No one is exempt from problems. They even come to Brother Hagin.

In case you don't know, Rev. Kenneth E. Hagin happens to be my dad. Even though Rev. Hagin is recognized as a faith teacher, frustrations in life come to him too.

Do you know why? Because he's a man, and the devil brings accusations and frustrations against every person on the face of this earth. But it's what Brother Hagin does in the midst of the frustrations of life that makes all the difference. He has learned to look only to God and focus on His Word, not on the problems.

When you only look to God and His Word, you can rise above your problems every time! It's what you do with frustrations and problems that determines whether you enjoy victory or suffer in defeat!

What do *you* do in the face of your problems? Do you look to God and magnify *Him*? Or do you look at the problem and magnify the problem? That's what determines whether you will have victory or defeat.

You are the one who decides if you will ever walk in God's victory plan for your life. You alone hold the key to victory or defeat in your situation.

Learn how to turn defeat into victory! There's never any reason for you to be defeated. God's Word promises you the victory — always! But you need to know that *you* are the one who determines your outcome, not God because He's always faithful to His promises.

Your pastor doesn't hold the key to your defeat or victory. Your friends don't hold the key to your victory. *You* hold the key, and only *you* can use that key to determine your victory or defeat in every situation you face. What are you going to do about the problems that confront you? When are you going to use your key to victory — the promises in God's Word?

I can pray for you; your neighbor, your momma, daddy, grandma, and grandpa can all pray for you. Yes, you can get Uncle Johnny and Aunt Susie and all the kids to pray for you. But you're still not going to get any long-lasting relief from your problem until you take the keys in God's Word and use them to unlock the door to victory!

You will be defeated until you decide, "I'm going to be a victor! I'm going to win because Jesus promised me the victory in every circumstance. I will not allow the devil to have the authority in this situation because Jesus defeated him at the Cross!"

Then you need to pick up the keys of your authority and start using your faith to believe the promises of God. It's up to you — no one else.

The children of Israel had to come to a point of decision whether or not they would believe God's words to them: "Stand still and see the salvation of the Lord upon you." Actually, because of all their doubt and unbelief, they would have been in a mess if God hadn't been merciful to them.

Without God's mercy, the Israelites would have died right there at the Red Sea. But, really, Moses began preaching faith in God to the Israelites, and he told them to trust in God rather than in their circumstances.

When the Israelites finally changed their outlook, stood still, and looked to God to deliver them, one of the most amazing miracles in all of the Bible took place. The waters of the Red Sea parted and dry land appeared.

Now I've heard some say that the sea only parted far enough for the people to walk through single file. As if that would make it any less of a miracle!

It would have taken *days* to get two million people, all their belongings, and all their livestock across the Red Sea if they had only walked single file. There was no time for that.

No, when those waters rolled back, there was enough dry land for thousands to go through at once! God doesn't do anything halfway.

Others say that the Red Sea was only a few inches deep, so it was no problem for the children of Israel to walk through. If that were true, then we're talking about a greater miracle than the parting of the Red Sea! That would mean all of Pharaoh's army along with their horses and chariots were drowned in only a few inches of water!

Don't Negate God's Miracle-Working Power

You see, people who are filled with doubt and unbelief want to negate God's miracle-working power. But, friends, there's no explaining away the awesome power of God. He's the same God today as He was back then. He's still just as ready as He's ever been to exercise His miracle-working power to deliver His people!

I want you to see something that's important in the account of the Red Sea crossing. The Israelites did not defeat or stop their enemies themselves. *God* wanted to fight this battle for them! The Lord was going to defeat the enemy all by Himself.

You see, when you're walking in God's victory plan, God performs miraculous wonders for you. All you have to do is keep on walking in obedience and faith!

As the Israelites walked through the Red Sea on dry ground, their enemies were still in hot pursuit. But the same circumstances which had threatened to engulf the children of Israel ended up destroying their enemy! The waters swallowed up Pharoah's army, and they were no more.

God will do that for you too! He's no respecter of persons (Acts 10:34). If you'll stand still and trust in God, the very circumstances that seem to spell sure defeat for you will bring defeat to the enemy!

You'll see the power of God work on your behalf, and you'll walk away from that situation leaving the enemy in the dust behind you. However, that will never take place as long as you stand around complaining and wondering if God's power will work for you. Have faith in God's victory plan!

It's up to you whether you will be defeated spiritually or whether you will come out the victor. You don't have to be defeated because defeat is *not* part of God's victory plan.

Yes, there's turmoil, oppression, domestic trouble, and sickness and disease arrayed against all of us. The devil is raging; there's no doubt about it. He may not be very smart, but he's got enough sense to recognize that his time is almost up. That's why he's doing all he can to take everyone in the church down with him.

However, you don't have to be one of his casualties. For example, when your boat on life's sea is about to capsize with domestic problems, when a sea of sickness and disease lies in your path, stand your ground believing God's Word. You can't walk in God's victory plan without the Word!

Remember the words the Lord spoke to the children of Israel in Second Chronicles 16:9:

2 CHRONICLES 16:9
9   For the eyes of the Lord run to and fro throughout the whole earth, to shew himself strong IN THE BEHALF OF THEM WHOSE HEART IS PERFECT TOWARD HIM. . . .

God is searching the whole earth. He's looking for those who will walk in faith in the victory He's already provided for them by standing on the promises in His Word. The promises of God bring victory!

God is not looking for those who are complaining and griping. Griping never wins you the victory. It only hinders you spiritually.

God is looking for those who trust in Him. He's looking for those who will rely on His promises. They are the ones He will demonstrate His mighty delivering power to. Let me tell you — when you stand your ground in faith, things get exciting!

Now I'm not saying that faith in the Word will keep you from ever having problems. In fact, I get a little disgusted with some people who hear a few messages on faith and think that automatically makes them faith giants. They go off saying things like, "*I'm* never going to have any more trials or troubles because *I'm* living by faith! *I* confess the Word!"

All I can say is that people like that must think they know more than the Apostle Paul who wrote more than half the New Testament. I read in the New Testament that Paul was beaten, stoned, and left for dead. He was shipwrecked, imprisoned, and in constant perils from robbers and fellow countrymen.

Paul was a man of great faith, yet he encountered difficult situations. His faith didn't keep the trials from coming. But his faith did enable him to overcome every one of those trials! You can read for yourself that Paul wrote that he *always* triumphed in Christ Jesus!

None of us is ever going to reach the place in this life where we will never have any problems. You can't find Scriptures that promise you a problem-free life because Satan is the god of this world (2 Cor. 4:4).

But you can stand in faith and watch God take you through those problems as more than a conqueror!

God cares for us even in the midst of every problem, frustration, or negative circumstance. Thank God, God is a merciful God! We would all be in a mess if God weren't merciful.

God wants to work on our behalf, but we have to allow Him to help us.

We have to trust Him. God looks to see what we're going to do in the midst of trouble.

Your Choice — Fear or Faith

The question each one of us will have to answer when problems come our way is this: Are we going to get fearful? Or are we going to have faith in God? We need to realize that God in His wisdom already looked ahead and saw every circumstance that would try to come against us — and He already planned for our victory!

Are we going to walk in God's victory plan for our lives? Are we going to stand up like soldiers of the Cross and valiantly stride forth in faith, boldly declaring, "I shall overcome in Jesus' Name. I will not be defeated! I shall have victory! Jesus has already purchased it for me, and the enemy will not defeat me."

What are *you* doing in the midst of your circumstances? Are you trusting God and believing in the promises in His Word? Or are you believing your circumstances will prevail and overcome you?

Get on God's victory side! How do you do that? By getting in agreement with His Word! You can have victory! Determine that you will stand firm in your faith on God's promises. Then expect to see the salvation of the Lord!

All you have to do to overcome any problem is to believe God's Word instead of the problem. Then stand firm in your faith. Don't back down from the devil. You have authority over him. You can stand up to the devil's attack with the Word of God, and he has to back down because of the authority in the Word.

God wants to deliver us in every circumstance we face. He wants to set us free. He told us in Hebrews 4:16 that we have a right to come boldly before His throne to obtain mercy and grace to help us in time of every need. Therefore, we have a right to confidently expect that God will use His power to deliver us!

What do you need from God? Whatever it is, He's got it for you. But you've got to take the key — your faith in His Word — and lay hold of your victory. Many people don't put their faith out for anything, so they never receive anything!

You need to declare to God: "Father, I am standing on Your Word. I've done all that Your Word tells me to do, so now I am standing in faith. I *expect* to see Your salvation in this situation."

Victory or defeat — it's your choice! Which one will you receive? Will you trust in the circumstances you see all around you? Or will you trust in God's Word? It's not God's decision to make. The choice is up to you!

Chapter 5
Death or Deliverance?

There's only one way to receive deliverance, healing, or whatever it is that you want from God, and that is to believe God's Word and go after your answer like a drowning man after his last breath! Those who make half-hearted, lukewarm attempts at believing God for deliverance will end up in failure.

Your defeat or victory is up to you. You can choose to wallow in defeat, or you can choose to walk in the victory that God has already provided for you in Christ.

In the Bible we find four lepers who had every opportunity to choose defeat. Their city, Samaria, was ravaged by famine. They were hopeless lepers, outcasts in their society, doomed to die.

But they made a choice. They determined to do what they could to live. Really, they activated their faith to do *something* to stay alive.

2 KINGS 7:1-5
1 Then Elisha said, Hear ye the word of the Lord; Thus saith the Lord, To morrow about this time shall a measure of fine flour be sold for a shekel, and two measures of barley for a shekel, in the gate of Samaria.

2   Then a lord on whose hand the king leaned
answered the man of God, and said, Behold, if the
Lord would make windows in heaven, might this
thing be? And he said, Behold, thou shalt see it
with thine eyes, but shalt not eat thereof.
3   And there were four leprous men at the enter-
ing in of the gate: and they said one to another,
WHY SIT WE HERE UNTIL WE DIE?
4   If we say, We will enter into the city, then the
famine is in the city, and we shall die there: and if
we sit still here, we die also. Now therefore come,
and let us fall unto the host of the Syrians: if they
save us alive, we shall live; and if they kill us, we
shall but die.
5   And THEY ROSE UP IN THE TWILIGHT, TO
GO UNTO THE CAMP OF THE SYRIANS: and
when they were come to the uttermost part of the
camp of Syria, behold, there was no man there.

In this passage of Scripture, it is recorded that the
entire city of Samaria had been shut off and was surrounded by the Syrian army. The Syrian army had iso-
lated the city by cutting off its food supply and its
contact with the outside world.

The result was that from the loftiest halls of the
king's palace to the lowliest dirt floors of the poorest
peasant, famine stalked Samaria. Whether rich or poor,
there was no difference. Each man was the same. Death
threatened them all.

You see, the Israelites — God's people — had drifted
away from the Lord, so that gave the enemy an opportunity to overrun them. When God's people are in dis-
obedience, it lifts the hand of God's blessing and
protection from them.

In Second Kings 7:1 and 2, Elisha prophesied that
the famine would halt suddenly with the provision of an
abundance of food. One of the king's helpers mocked the
prophet's words by saying, *"Behold, if the Lord would
make windows in heaven, might this thing be? . . ."*
(2 Kings 7:2).

Elisha replied, *". . . Behold, thou shalt see it with
thine eyes, but shalt not eat thereof"* (2 Kings 7:2). When
the word of the Lord came true, this man died; the people trampled him to get to the supply of food.

But the four lepers didn't hear Elijah's prophecy
because they lived outside the city. So as far as they
were concerned, they had no hope. With disease rav-
aging their bodies and hopelessness tormenting their
minds, these lepers walked about as dead men.

These four lepers were surrounded by death. Death
not only ravaged their bodies through disease, but death
stalked the city through famine. Also, the enemy surrounded the city, just waiting to bring death, destruction, and the sword to every one of the Israelites.

These four lepers were in a no-win situation
because death threatened them from every side. From
within and without, death was quickly closing in all
around them. But in the face of total destruction, they
looked at the reality of their situation and asked themselves a crucial question: *". . . why sit we here until we
die?"* (2 Kings 7:3).

They reasoned that if they went into the city, they
would die by famine. If they just sat there, they'd die
anyway from starvation and disease. At least if they

went into the Syrian camp, they'd have a chance to survive. Maybe their enemy would have mercy on them and let them live; they might even give them something to eat!

The lepers were in a hopeless situation! It seemed as though there was no way out. Some of us have faced hopeless situations too.

For example, you know you're in a hopeless situation when doctors look at you and tell you, "Your disease is incurable! You've only got a few months to live"! Many times when people are in that kind of a hopeless situation, they turn to God.

It seems that hopelessness brings people to the reality of believing God more quickly than anything else. People in hopeless situations often seem to get delivered faster than others for the simple reason that they turn to God completely, realizing that He is their only hope.

It seems that sometimes until people reach the hopeless stage, they still have their faith in the arm of flesh. If only they'd realize that their hope needs to be in God and in His Word.

Life or Death — The Choice Is Yours

Death and destruction or victory and life! It's up to you. You are the one who has the final say-so. Are you going to believe God's Word and stand your ground on it? Or are you going to believe the negative circumstances?

You alone have the final word on every situation you face. What will you believe? You can come out defeated, or you can come out the victor. No one else can make that choice for you. You choose between defeat and victory by whether or not you take your stand on God's Word.

Actually, people should turn to God first instead of turning to man first, but thank God for His mercy! Thousands have turned to God when all else has failed, and He has been faithful to reveal His power to all who call upon His Name (Ps. 86:5; Rom. 10:12).

The four lepers in Second Kings chapter 7 found themselves in a hopeless situation. Cast out of the city because of their disease, they could do nothing but sit and wait to die.

You say, "That's a sad story!" But what's really sad is that many people today are doing the same thing both spiritually and physically — they're just sitting around waiting to die. Yet they have the power of deliverance within their grasp! Why? Because God's saving power is available to anyone who will seek Him.

The devil wants you to sit around waiting in a state of despair and hopelessness. As long as he can keep you from acting in faith on God's Word, he can keep you defeated.

By doing nothing, you are accepting defeat and hopelessness. When you refuse to act in faith, unbelief and its consequences will run rampant in your life.

But the Word of God says that Jesus Christ came to the world to bring hope for sick and suffering humanity.

Jesus came to give you *life*, not *death*. He came to show God's delivering power to mankind.

Everywhere Jesus went, He taught the Word and instilled faith in people. Those who *exercised* their faith and *acted* on Jesus' words were healed.

If you are sick and suffering or hopeless and depressed, I want you to know there is hope for you! You don't have to die. You don't have to wallow around in depression and futility.

And you don't have to suffer with sickness and disease or live in torment either. You can be healed, and you can be delivered from *all* torment.

Don't give in to the devil who tries to preach his defeat and despair. Turn to Jesus Christ who was manifested to destroy the works of the enemy (1 John 3:8).

Some people say, "Well, if it's God's will, He'll heal me." Or they say, "If God wants to, He'll deliver me." I don't know whether those statements are a cop-out or whether that's just a lack of knowledge. I think it's probably a little of both!

Why? Because God has already healed and delivered every person on the face of this earth through Jesus' death, burial, and resurrection. Now you just need to accept His Word and receive your healing and deliverance.

But I think some Christians just want everyone else to try to get their healing for them. They seem to want God to do everything for them, so *they* don't have to put forth any effort to believe Him.

I'm sorry to say, but there are lazy people in this world who just want someone else to do all their work for them. And I believe that in some cases this same spirit of laziness has gotten over into the church!

It takes some effort to exercise your faith!

In the natural, people can just lie around and get fat because they don't want to exercise. It takes a lot of effort to exercise! The flesh doesn't like exercise because it takes discipline.

In the same way, some people are never delivered because they never put forth any action to help themselves. They never do anything to receive healing, yet they whine and cry and wonder why they don't receive anything from God.

They whine, "Well, the Bible says I can be healed. So *maybe* I can."

Yes, you can be healed! But the Bible doesn't say, "Sit down and do nothing." It says, "Take your faith and stand against the wiles of the devil!"

You're supposed to stand against negative circumstances! You're supposed to stand against the devil's symptoms and strategies in your life! The message of the Bible is, "Get your faith into action by believing God!"

Friend, I'm going to tell you a little secret. It takes some effort and discipline to exercise your faith and to walk in the Word of God. You have to make yourself read the Word even when you don't feel like it. You've got to stand in faith even when you'd rather just be lazy and take a nap!

Sometimes you've got to make yourself praise God when you would rather sit down and watch television. You've got to discipline yourself to keep yourself spiritually fit, and discipline is something most people don't like.

We live in a day and age when everything is fast and easy — push-button controls, fast-food restaurants, and instant success. But with God there are no push-button controls. There is no spiritual autopilot or cruise control.

You must operate in the spiritual realm daily — hour by hour and day by day — because the minute you try to put your spiritual life on "cruise control," the devil will take over and run you into the ground.

The Word of God tells us to be continually on guard against the devil's schemes and devices (1 Peter 5:8). We need to be aware of Satan's devices and stay prepared!

Why Sit in Doubt Till You Die?

Jesus came to destroy the works of Satan. He came to deliver all who will believe on His Name. That's why you don't have to just sit around in doubt and hopelessness waiting to die! Look at the Word and you'll see that you've already been delivered from the devil's oppression.

ACTS 10:38
38 How God anointed Jesus of Nazareth with the Holy Ghost and with power: who went about

doing good, and HEALING ALL THAT WERE OPPRESSED OF THE DEVIL; for God was with him.

Jesus came to set men free, which includes freedom from sickness and disease. In Psalm 103:3, it says that God ". . . *forgiveth all thine iniquities; who HEALETH ALL THY DISEASES.*"

Why do we just accept the first part of that Scripture about forgiveness, but we don't *act in faith* on the rest of it about healing?

We accept the part about the forgiveness of our sins, and we exercise our faith when we go to God to ask His forgiveness. For example, people will readily say, "Sure, Jesus *forgives* all our sins." But in the same Scripture, it also says, He "*heals* all our diseases."

The same God who forgives our sins also heals our diseases. Why not accept all of that Scripture instead of just part of it? Jesus has already made every provision for your healing. So "Why sit we here till we die?"

1 PETER 2:24
24 Who his own self bare our sins in his own body on the tree, that we, being dead to sins, should live unto righteousness: BY WHOSE STRIPES YE WERE HEALED.

MATTHEW 8:16,17
16 When the even was come, they brought unto him [Jesus] many that were possessed with devils: and he cast out the spirits with his word, and HEALED ALL THAT WERE SICK:
17 That it might be fulfilled which was spoken by Esaias the prophet, saying, HIMSELF TOOK OUR INFIRMITIES, AND BARE OUR SICKNESSES.

Yes, Jesus died for our sins, but He also died for our diseases. It was the same Calvary. It was the same trial of the Cross. And it was the same Jesus who suffered so that we might have life and have it more abundantly (John 10:10). Jesus promised us abundant life, so "Why sit we here till we die?"

Jesus didn't suffer and die so we could just have new life in the spiritual realm. He also died on the Cross so we could be healed in our physical bodies as we live for God down here on this earth.

Most of us know that Jesus redeemed us from sin, sickness, and disease. But how many of us are exercising our authority over sickness and disease in our bodies? How many of us are kicking Satan out of the circumstances in our lives that are trying to bring us into bondage?

You can do something about your circumstances! You don't just have to sit around and wait in depression to die or be defeated. God is still on the throne! God has already done something about your sickness and disease! He's already done something about hopelessness and depression. He sent Jesus to heal and deliver you.

So let me ask you this question, "Why not do something about your situation?" Don't just sit around doing nothing! *Apply God's Word to your situation.* Get your faith going!

That's what these lepers did. Those four men sitting outside the gate of Samaria had enough sense to get up and get their faith working. They got their faith in action by saying, "We don't have anything to lose! We might as well go up to the enemy camp."

Before they put their faith to work, all they could see was the grave. They felt like one way or another, they were bound to die.

Have you ever felt like that — like there was no hope for you? That's when you need to get your faith activated because the Word can bring you life!

Don't sit around waiting for the devil to kill you with sickness and disease! And don't sit around waiting for the devil to strangle you with his negative circumstances either! Get your faith into action. Believe God's Word. Act on it! What have you got to lose?

You're going to have to activate your faith just like these lepers did. They started activating their faith by what they said: "Let's get up and go!" You're going to have to do something to release your faith.

You can express your faith with faith-filled words. So what are you *saying* about your situation? Are you speaking God's Word out of your mouth? Or are you creating more problems for yourself by speaking negative words?

Begin to turn your faith loose by what you say. Speak the Word instead of the problem. You can begin to get your faith activated with faith-filled words. Ask yourself, *Why should I just sit here till I die? Why should I sit here and do nothing and be defeated?*

You're going to have to do something to act in faith. Sometimes you can act in faith by doing something you couldn't do before. Sometimes it's just as simple as speaking faith-filled words out of your mouth. Sometimes you get your faith activated by praising God that He's heard and answered your prayers.

There are all kinds of ways you can demonstrate your faith in action. These lepers demonstrated their faith by getting up and acting in all the faith they could muster.

You have to realize that these lepers were in the same desperate situation some of us have been in before. Anyone who has ever been sick or needs to be delivered by the power of God has to make the choice whether to give up or to persevere in faith.

These lepers had nothing to lose, so they embarked upon a mission of faith that seemed reckless. It's a good thing the lepers didn't listen to the king's counsel and the people inside the city. They probably would have told the lepers, "Don't go to the enemy camp. You'll be destroyed."

You see, sometimes people will try to talk you out of your faith. Some of you started to get hold of God's Word. When you did, maybe your relatives, some preachers, or even some of your friends tried to talk you out of God's blessings.

Let other people do what they want to, but *you* grab hold of God's Word and go on to victory! Let others stay in defeat if they want to, but you take God's Word and walk in God's victory plan for your life!

Don't just sit outside the gate of God's blessing. You come boldly before the throne of grace, and present what you need before your Heavenly Father. Just base your requests on His Word — because His Word can't return to Him without producing blessings in your life (Isa. 55:11).

It was still twilight when these lepers rose up to receive their victory while those in the city slept. Let others go ahead and sleep — but *you* rise up in faith!

2 KINGS 7:5
5 And they rose up in the twilight, to go unto the camp of the Syrians: and when they were come to the uttermost part of the camp of Syria, behold, there was no man there.

The lepers probably couldn't see very far as they marched on in the night. Can't you just imagine these four bedraggled men, rising up in the twilight of the early morning? It's hard to see when it's still dark out.

Even though they probably couldn't see very far down the road, at least they weren't just sitting around waiting to perish. They were acting out their faith by marching down that road to victory.

Now get this picture. Four sick, tired, weak, hungry lepers, walking along, probably dragging their feet as they went. At any moment, the enemy could have killed them on the road and taken their lives. But they marched on in faith anyway.

2 KINGS 7:6-8
6 For the Lord had made the host of the Syrians to hear a noise of chariots, and a noise of horses, even the noise of a great host: and they said one to another, Lo, the king of Israel hath hired against us the kings of the Hittites, and the kings of the Egyptians, to come upon us.

> 7 Wherefore they arose and fled in the twilight, and left their tents, and their horses, and their asses, even the camp as it was, and fled for their life.
>
> 8 And when these lepers came to the uttermost part of the camp, they went into one tent, and did eat and drink, and carried thence silver, and gold, and raiment, and went and hid it; and came again, and entered into another tent, and carried thence also, and went and hid it.

As they walked along, God caused the enemy to hear a great noise, and the Syrians said, ". . . *Lo, the king of Israel hath hired against us the kings of the Hittites, and the kings of the Egyptians, to come upon us*" (2 Kings 7:6).

Now get hold of this and get ready to shout. Four bedraggled sick men walking down the road became the catalyst that caused the word of the Lord through Elisha to come to pass: ". . . *Thus saith the Lord, To morrow about this time shall a measure of fine flour be sold for a shekel, and two measures of barley for a shekel, in the gate of Samaria*" (2 Kings 7:1).

Friend, when you get up and decide to do something in faith about your situation, you might be a catalyst, not only in your life, but in the lives of others. You do not know the chain reaction that can be set off by your rising up and coming to Jesus in faith.

These four disease-ridden men were probably wasting away. I imagine because of their disease, none of these men weighed more than 130 pounds. Yet these four seemingly hopeless men were used mightily by God. If God can use four weak lepers who weren't even born again, how much more can He use *you*!

Evidently God turned up the volume on these lepers' footsteps as they dragged their feet along the road, so it sounded to the Syrians like a great host was coming after them! Four hopeless men with God as their Helper sounded like a battalion of horsemen in hot pursuit. Somehow God made them sound like an army in full charge swooping down on the enemy camp.

The Syrians ran in terror and left all their silver, gold, and clothes in their tents. By the time the lepers came into camp, the enemy had fled. Those four bedraggled lepers plundered that camp and came away rich with silver and gold!

Then just like Elisha had prophesied, flour and barley were sold very cheaply at the gate of Samaria (2 Kings 7:1). The spoil became so plentiful that ". . . *a measure of fine flour . . . sold for a shekel, and two measures of barley for a shekel, in the gate of Samaria*" (2 Kings 7:1).

This was at the same gate where the lepers had sat begging before they finally made the decision, "We're not going to sit here and die! We're going to get up and do something about our situation!" And they headed off for the Syrian camp.

If God could do this for these poor beggars, just think what God can do with your faith in His Word! God's got every answer you'll ever need. Four bedraggled, leprous men changed the course of this battle. And these four men — outcasts from society — were the catalyst that caused the prophet's word to come to pass.

God can use your faith in His Word as a catalyst to change the course of circumstances too! With God, you don't ever need to be a victim; you can be a victor!

Those Syrians took off so fast in fear that they left everything behind! They left their swords, their spears, the silver and gold, their food — and they ran for their lives from four hungry, sick men.

If God can make the enemy run in terror from four sick, tired, worn-out lepers, just think what He can do with a Church that's been redeemed and washed in the blood of Jesus!

Just think what God could do with you because you're in Christ! If you only knew it, every time you use Jesus' Name in faith, the enemy runs from you in fear — just at the mention of that Name! No wonder the devil works overtime against the Church. He knows that if we ever find out who we are and what we have in Christ, he's had it!

When the lepers walked into the camp, they looked around and didn't see anyone. They peeked in the food tent, and they went in, sat down, and started eating. It had been a long time since they'd eaten so well.

Then they went into another tent and began carrying off all the silver, gold, and raiment, and hid their spoils. Sure, they were storing up all the goods. Why not? They're the ones who delivered the nation of Israel!

Friends, Jesus Christ has already driven the devil out of *your* inheritance. All you've got to do is come into the camp and get the gold and the silver — your inheritance in Christ — and pick up your royal robes! Get ahold of this! The enemy is defeated! When you speak the Word, the enemy runs out of your camp in terror. He takes his hands off your possessions — your silver, gold, and your raiment. So don't be afraid to speak the Word boldly so you can walk in to God's victory plan for your life.

Walk into the enemy's camp wearing the full armor of God, take the Name of Jesus, and by the blood of the Lamb, drive that thief off your property! This is God's victory plan for you.

These disease-ridden lepers were bold. And they weren't even born again or filled with the Spirit of God! Yet look what they accomplished just by faith and action! Can you imagine the ecstasy of those four lepers when they walked into the Syrian camp and everyone had fled! They walked around that camp and took whatever they needed and wanted.

Hide in God's Invincible Word

You need to do the same thing. Your goods have stayed too long in the enemy's camp. You need to get bold because you're armed with the Word of God. Sure, you're nothing in yourself. But in Christ — full of the Word of God — God and you are invincible!

The lepers finally realized that they needed to tell the others about all the spoil; they didn't want to be

God's Victory Plan

selfish. They said to one another, "Our family and friends back in Samaria are dying, and we've got food and clothing. We've got to go help them."

2 KINGS 7:9-12
9 Then they said one to another, We do not well: this day is a day of good tidings, and we hold our peace: if we tarry till the morning light, some mischief will come upon us: now therefore come, that we may go and tell the king's household.
10 So they came and called unto the porter of the city: and they told them, saying, We came to the camp of the Syrians, and, behold, there was no man there, neither voice of man, but horses tied, and asses tied, and the tents as they were.
11 And he called the porters; and they told it to the king's house within.
12 And the king arose in the night, and said unto his servants, I will now shew you what the Syrians have done to us. They know that we be hungry; therefore are they gone out of the camp to hide themselves in the field, saying, When they come out of the city, we shall catch them alive, and get into the city.

The lepers ran back to Samaria and beat on the city gate. They called out, "Hey! Do you want something to eat? You want some gold and silver? The Syrians have fled and their camp is empty. All their horses and chariots are gone."

Do you know what? The people in that city were just like some friends, relatives, and unsaved people today. You try to go back and tell them all the good things that the Lord has done for you, and some of them don't believe it. They don't understand that they, too, have an inheritance in Christ!

The King said, "I don't believe it! That's just a trick to get us down there so the Syrians can destroy us."

You see, Elisha had prophesied about this victory, but the Israelites still didn't believe. They weren't expecting *God* to set them free. They didn't even realize that God was offering them deliverance through four lepers.

> **2 KINGS 7:13-16**
> **13 And one of his servants answered and said, Let some take, I pray thee, five of the horses that remain, which are left in the city . . . and let us send and see.**
> **14 They took therefore two chariot horses; and the king sent after the host of the Syrians, saying, Go and see.**
> **15 And they went after them unto Jordan: and, lo, ALL THE WAY WAS FULL OF GARMENTS AND VESSELS, WHICH THE SYRIANS HAD CAST AWAY IN THEIR HASTE. And the messengers returned, and told the king.**
> **16 And the people went out, and spoiled the tents of the Syrians. So a measure of fine flour was sold for a shekel, and two measures of barley for a shekel, according to the word of the Lord.**

I'm sure those lepers became the heroes of the day when they announced to the Israelites that they had plundered the Syrian camp! Their faith paid off! There's always a reward for faith in God.

You see, the Lord always brings His Word to pass, and He can use the most unlikely people to do it — including you and me!

But the fellow who didn't believe God's Word through Elisha had said, *". . . Behold, if the Lord would make windows in heaven, might this thing be?"* The prophet answered him and said, *". . . Behold, thou shalt see it with thine eyes, but shalt not eat thereof"* (2 Kings 7:2).

Although the Word of the Lord was fulfilled, there was a penalty for this man's doubt and unbelief. He never lived to see Elisha's prophecy fulfilled because he was trampled at the gate (2 Kings 7:17)!

Some of your friends and relatives may not believe what God is telling you either. But don't worry about it if they don't want to go on with God. Pray for them, of course. But it's their decision if they don't want to walk with God. You've done your part by telling them about God's wonderful healing and delivering power.

So go tell your message of God's delivering power where people are hungry. There are people who want to hear what you have to say!

Friends, I want to encourage you to get up and do something about your situation. Few people have ever received deliverance who haven't marched valiantly for it, armed with the Word of God. Few people have ever been delivered from sickness and affliction who have not had to stand their ground on the Word and march in faith toward the victory!

Acting on Faith-Filled Words

There was a man in the New Testament who had no hope either. He was lame and doomed to live a life sitting by the side of the road begging for food. He had no hope for his future. He had no cause to rejoice at anything. But he changed his situation because he chose victory!

How? He acted in faith on the faith-filled words he heard. Faith comes by hearing, and faith demands a response — an act. The lame man at the Gate called Beautiful heard words of faith and did something about his situation.

ACTS 3:1-10
1 Now Peter and John went up together into the temple at the hour of prayer, being the ninth hour.
2 And a certain man lame from his mother's womb was carried, whom they laid daily at the gate of the temple which is called Beautiful, to ask alms of them that entered into the temple;
3 Who seeing Peter and John about to go into the temple asked an alms.
4 And Peter, fastening his eyes upon him with John, said, Look on us.
5 And he gave heed unto them, expecting to receive something of them.
6 Then Peter said, Silver and gold have I none; but such as I have give I thee: In the name of Jesus Christ of Nazareth rise up and walk.
7 And he took him by the right hand, and lifted him up: and immediately his feet and ankle bones received strength.
8 And he leaping up stood, and walked, and entered with them into the temple, walking, and leaping, and praising God.

**9 And all the people saw him walking and prais-
ing God:
10 And they knew that it was he which sat for
alms at the Beautiful gate of the temple: and they
were filled with wonder and amazement at that
which had happened unto him.**

Peter and John walked through the Gate called
Beautiful to go down to the temple to pray. A lame fellow sat there at the gate begging. He was probably
shaking his tin cup trying to get people to drop money
into it.

I remember when I was a kid, I used to go into
downtown Dallas with Mom. There was a store down
there that sold a little bit of everything. It even had an
old-fashioned soda fountain.

A man always sat on the corner by that store. I still
remember him. He sold pencils in an old tin cup that
he'd shake around so those pencils would rattle. You
were supposed to drop in some money and take a pen-
cil. Some of the mean little neighborhood boys would
run by and steal his pencils and not drop any money in
the cup.

But he just sat there day after day, shaking that cup
all the time, begging. He was afflicted with some kind
of disease so that he couldn't walk. I imagine that the
lame man at the Gate called Beautiful was sort of in
the same situation.

As Peter and John walked through the Gate Beautiful, Peter looked down at the lame man, and said,
". . . Silver and gold have I none; but such as I have give

I thee: In the name of Jesus Christ of Nazareth rise up and walk" (Acts 3:6).

Most of the time, I think we miss the point of this account. Many times we give all the attention to Peter's statement: "Rise and walk." But do you know Peter's faith statement is not altogether what brought the victory for this man?

Peter's statement of faith is part of what got him healed. But what really healed that lame man was that he immediately got up and acted on his own faith! The minute that man put action to his faith in Peter's statement, strength came into his feet and ankle bones.

You see, the lame man had something to do with his healing. He responded to Peter's words in faith. Then he put action to his faith. He made the effort to get up. Why? Because he *believed* the words that Peter spoke, so he did something about it.

You can do the same thing. You just need to activate your faith in God's Word! What action can you put to your faith? How can you get your faith activated?

Start by confessing God's Word for what you need. Then praise and thank God for the answer by faith (Mark 11:24). That's how you begin to act out your faith. If you need healing, begin to do something you couldn't do before.

For example, I read an article about some healing preachers back in the '50s. These ministers went to pray for a man who had been in bed for eight months with arthritis. He'd been almost totally incapacitated all those months.

They prayed for him, and the power of God came into that place. The man said to those ministers, "I feel like I should jump out of this bed and run around the house."

The ministers encouraged him to do that as an act of faith. "Do it!" they said. "Act in faith that you're healed."

But the man didn't budge. He was reluctant to demonstrate his faith — he wouldn't *act* healed. What happened? He didn't receive his healing. Even though the power of God came mightily upon that man, he wouldn't take a step of faith, so God had nothing to work with on his behalf. Faith pleases God (Heb. 11:6).

In that article, one of those ministers who was present that day, said, "I believe if he had just responded to the urging of the Spirit of God on the inside of him, he would have been made completely whole."

Many times people are prayed for and when the power of God comes on them, they feel an urge to do something, but they don't yield to it. They just sit there. They don't understand that they have to *act* on their faith.

I know about another man who was prayed for because he was paralyzed. This man acted on his faith. He didn't just sit around and wait to die. He said, "I felt the power of God on me, and I just felt like I ought to do something. I felt like I ought to try to move something."

Now this man was completely paralyzed. The only thing that he could move was his little finger. So he started moving that one little finger, and he kept moving that finger, until soon he could move two or three fingers.

As he kept his faith activated by moving his fingers, it wasn't long before he could move his whole hand. Then by keeping his faith activated, before long he was completely healed.

But, you see, he started out by trying to do something he couldn't do before. He put some action to the power of God that was in manifestation. He activated his faith by doing something. He didn't just sit around and do nothing.

"Why sit here till we die?" Faith is an act. This man didn't focus on what he couldn't do; he focused on what he could do! That's faith in action.

Faith in the Impossible

I know what it's like to trust God for healing when everything looks impossible. I had an incurable ear disease when I was fifteen years old. I'd been in church and heard the Word of God preached all my life, and I'd seen the power of God demonstrated.

So at fifteen years old, I had to make the decision whether I was going to live the rest of my life with a disease that was eating up the inside of my ear, or whether I was going to receive deliverance.

I made up my mind that I was going to walk in faith. Now I'm not telling you to do what I did. You have to do what you believe God wants you to do. But I had to believe God. So I prayed a simple prayer asking God to heal my ear, and then I had to believe that God *heard* and *answered* me.

For two weeks I believed God. I hung on to the Scriptures about healing. I kept confessing, "I'm healed by the power of God." The doctor had told me never to put my head under water again, and especially never to go swimming. I'd been told to move out of a damp climate and live somewhere in a dry climate like the deserts of Arizona or New Mexico.

But in gym class that day at school, I was supposed to dive into the pool and swim the length of the pool underwater. As I dove into the shallow end of the pool, my mind screamed at me, *You're crazy! You know how bad your ear hurts!*

And it did hurt! That infection caused the inside of my ear to swell up. I'd just barely touch that ear when I rolled over at night, and I'd come straight up in bed, it hurt so bad.

So that day as I acted in faith, my mind screamed at me, but my heart told me, *You're healed by the power of God. Now act like it!* I put some action to my prayers. I acted on my faith.

When I dove into that pool, I swam all the way to the other end underwater. After swimming the entire length of that Olympic-sized swimming pool, when I broke the surface of that water, I heard a "Pop!" inside my head. I said, "Thank God! All the pain is gone."

Some of the guys in the pool asked me, "What are you talking about?" I just said, "Never mind." They wouldn't have understood. Sometimes if you try to explain your healing or something supernatural that happened to you, people won't understand it, so they'll get you back in the arena of unbelief. It wasn't the proper time to try to explain it to my classmates.

But I'd made up my mind that I wasn't going to just sit around, do nothing, and lose my hearing because of this incurable disease.

Some of you are suffering with sickness and disease. Actually, some of you are going to die unless you experience the healing power of God. Others of you suffer with a chronic sickness or disease that's always with you. It's not terminal, but it's incurable.

You must make up your mind whether you're going to receive deliverance or whether you're going to sit and die. It's up to you. It's not up to God. Why sit there till you die?

Activate your faith on all those wonderful promises in God's Word. To do nothing is to die or fail. But when you act in faith on God's promise, you are saying, "I will not sit still and die. I will trust God."

Remember, *"Many are the afflictions of the righteous: but the Lord DELIVERETH him out of them ALL"* (Ps. 34:19).

Don't give up! Your faith in God will see you through! Just don't ever quit. For some people, it just seems like it's easy for them to quit. For other people, it seems like they just sort of have some kind of tenacity that won't let them quit in their faith.

My family is like that. We just seem to have a tenacity that won't let us quit. I always accepted a challenge, even as a kid. In high school my football coaches knew that challenges motivated me.

Sometimes they would challenge me by saying, "Now, Hagin, we know the guy you're going to guard tonight is better than you are. You're just not quite as good as he is." That would cause me to rise to the challenge and play all the harder!

In track, the coaches would tell me, "Now you just stay out of the way, and do the best you can because you're running against the big boys today."

They knew exactly what they were doing! They were challenging me to work even harder to win because they knew I wouldn't quit! I'd just dig my heels in and try even harder and run faster than I had ever done.

Something on the inside of me always made me want to rise to a challenge. I'd go out there and show them that I could not be stopped — and I wasn't about to quit!

Friend, I'm going to tell you something! I do the same thing today when I face the devil. I show the devil that I can't be stopped. He and his cohorts can't stop me, not because of who I am, but because of *whose* I am. I am a child of the living God!

I know that God's Word will carry me through. I don't claim to be perfect. I don't claim to be somebody big; all I claim to be is washed by the blood of the Lord Jesus Christ.

I know how to take my stand on the Word of God. I've said to God, "God, I know I am nothing in myself.

But I'm going to stand on Your Word that says I am an overcomer in Christ Jesus."

I've stood on the Word of God with tears running down my face, as I've determined to go on with God. I don't know how to give anything but 110 percent. If I play ball, I give it everything I've got. When I preach, I preach with everything I've got.

It's time that we learn that if we're going to go over with God, we can't be half-hearted, lukewarm, or uncommitted. We've got to walk with God with everything that we've got.

Grab hold of the Word of God like your life depends upon it — because it does. And God's Word will carry you to victory!

Jesus said, *"Heaven and earth shall pass away, but my words shall not pass away"* (Matt. 24:35). Do you see why it's so important to hold on to the Word? Since God's Word won't pass away, then speak it over your sickness or disease, your circumstances, or the fiery trial that's come to test you. Watch God's Word cause those negative circumstances to pass away!

God's Word is real, and the power of God is real. The same God who delivered those four lepers will set you free today wherever you live. It doesn't make any difference what circumstances you face. The power of God is available to you!

You must make up your mind. Are you going to sit there and die? Are you going to just sit there and let those circumstances rob you of God's blessings?

You've also got to use your faith to get up and go to Jesus. *Your faith releases the power of God in your situation.*

Chapter 6
Snatching Victory
From Defeat

Have you ever noticed in the Word of God that what seemed to be some of the greatest victories came out of what looked like utter defeat? That's what God in His Almighty power can do!

But do you know what made the difference in these situations? What the people believed! It was their faith in God that determined whether their outcome was victory or defeat.

Very often it can seem like the enemy has triumphed and gotten the upper hand over you. Sometimes all the circumstances look like the devil's got everything going his way, and you've got nothing going your way.

But then God comes along with His miracle-working power and upsets the devil's schemes. God takes what the devil meant for harm and turns the whole situation around! Nothing is too hard for God!

You may be facing a situation right now that's so dark, it seems like the enemy has ganged up on you. He may be trying to steal your joy and your triumph. But you don't have to let him get away with your victory. You can snatch victory out of defeat!

Delivered From the Fiery Trial

Great men and women of faith in the Old Testament became giants in faith because they learned exactly how to snatch victory out of defeat in every single situation! Let's look at some of those faith giants so we can see how to turn the devil's defeat into the Lord's victory.

The Book of Daniel is a good place to start.

DANIEL 3:1,3-6
1 Nebuchadnezzar the king made an image of gold, whose height was threescore cubits, and the breadth thereof six cubits: he set it up in the plain of Dura, in the province of Babylon. . . .
3 Then the princes, the governors, and captains, the judges, the treasurers, the counsellors, the sheriffs, and all the rulers of the provinces, were gathered together unto the dedication of the image that Nebuchadnezzar the king had set up; and they stood before the image that Nebuchadnezzar had set up.
4 Then an herald cried aloud, To you it is commanded, O people, nations, and languages,
5 That at what time ye hear the sound of the cornet, flute, harp, sackbut, psaltery, dulcimer, and all kinds of music, ye fall down and worship the golden image that Nebuchadnezzar the king hath set up:
6 And whoso falleth not down and worshippeth shall the same hour be cast into the midst of a burning fiery furnace.

Let me give you an account of what happened in this chapter. You know that King Nebuchadnezzar made a golden image, which was about ninety feet high and nine feet wide. He established it out on the plains, so he could have all his subjects assemble around it.

Then King Nebuchadnezzar called all the leaders of his people — the princes, governors, captains, judges, and counsellors — to gather around this image to worship it.

One of his dignitaries stood up among all the rulers of the provinces, and in a very loud voice, announced, "To you it is commanded, O people, when you hear the sound of the music to bow down and worship the golden image that King Nebuchadnezzar has set up."

You see, in Daniel's day, King Nebuchadnezzar was the head of the Babylonian Empire. And by commanding the people to worship one image, Nebuchadnezzar was trying to unify the different peoples in his kingdom. Of course, the image resembled the king!

But there were three Hebrew young men who didn't bow before the golden image. They had been taught not to worship any God except the Lord God, the true and living God.

DANIEL 3:14-19
14 Nebuchadnezzar spake and said unto them, Is it true, O Shadrach, Meshach, and Abed-nego, do not ye serve my gods, nor worship the golden image which I have set up?
15 Now if ye be ready that at what time ye hear the sound of the cornet, flute, harp, sackbut, psaltery, and dulcimer, and all kinds of music, ye

fall down and worship the image which I have
made; well: but if ye worship not, ye shall be cast
the same hour into the midst of a burning fiery
furnace; and who is that God that shall deliver you
out of my hands?
16 Shadrach, Meshach, and Abed-nego, answered
and said to the king, O Nebuchadnezzar, we are
not careful to answer thee in this matter.
17 If it be so, our God whom we serve is able to
deliver us from the burning fiery furnace, and he
will deliver us out of thine hand, O king.
18 But if not, be it known unto thee, O king, that
we will not serve thy gods, nor worship the golden
image which thou hast set up.
19 Then was Nebuchadnezzar full of fury, and the
form of his visage was changed against Shadrach,
Meshach, and Abed-nego: therefore he spake, and
commanded that they should heat the furnace one
seven times more than it was wont to be heated.

Actually, the king happened to like these three
young men. They were some of the best men in his
kingdom, so at first when they didn't bow and worship
this golden image, he wanted to give them another
chance. He wanted to give them the benefit of the
doubt. He didn't want to have to kill them.

So King Nebuchadnezzar said to the Hebrews,
"Maybe you didn't understand the royal decree. If you
don't bow your knee to the golden image I made, you're
going to burn in the fiery furnace." And he personally
explained to them what he expected them to do.

But these three young men had been taught that no
matter what happened, they were not to defile themselves by worshipping foreign idols and gods.

So they replied, "We do not have to defend ourselves to you, O King. Our God will take care of us." The *King James Version* says, *". . . We are not careful to answer thee in this matter"* (v. 16).

Then the three Hebrew children proclaimed their faith by saying, *". . . our God whom we serve is able to deliver us from the burning fiery furnace, and he will deliver us out of thine hand, O king"* (Dan. 3:17).

Whenever you make a statement of faith, you'd better be ready to back it up with a statement of commitment, or else your faith won't work! That's exactly what these three Hebrews did. Their statement of faith was that God would deliver them. Then in the next verse, they declared their statement of commitment.

DANIEL 3:18
18 . . . be it known unto thee, O king, that we will not serve thy gods, nor worship the golden image which thou hast set up.

You see, you can make all the faith statements you want to make, but unless you are ready to stand your ground and be committed to your faith in the face of all obstacles, your commitment is not going to work.

Christians love to talk about faith, but when you start talking about commitment, people don't like it. Why? Because with commitment comes responsibility.

We're living in a day and age when people don't want to be responsible for anything. I mean, some people will just walk by and watch while someone beats another person to death, and say, "I don't want to get involved!"

But commitment and faith go hand in hand. You'll never develop strong faith without also developing strong commitment to what you believe in.

Recently, my wife, Lynette, and I were in our car, and we were stopped at a major intersection, waiting for the traffic signal to change. Just as the light was about to change to green, I saw a car suddenly turn left in front of an oncoming vehicle, and they crashed into one another.

It was five o'clock in the afternoon during rush-hour traffic, and there were people everywhere. Several people saw the accident occur, but only two of us were willing to give our names to the policeman as witnesses!

One man was asked, "Did you see the accident?"

"Yes," he said.

"Will you be a witness to what you saw?"

"No," he replied, "I've got to go."

Many people don't want to make any commitments or get involved in anything. They don't want to be inconvenienced, and they sure don't want to have to testify in a court of law about something they've witnessed.

That same kind of spirit that's in the world has crept into the church. People just want to come to church, but they don't want to be committed, inconvenienced, or involved.

They just want a nice little sermon preached to them so they can go their way and enjoy their life. They just want to live in their own little world without any other annoyances or extra responsibilities.

Fear Weakens Faith

But weak commitment to the things of God creates weak faith! You can test how great your faith is by how strong your commitment is to God.

These three Hebrews children in Daniel 3 were committed to God! Even in the face of this fiery ordeal, they looked to God as their Deliverer. They weren't about to defile their faith by bowing down to the king's image.

Fear will cause you to get into doubt and unbelief, and it will weaken your faith in God. When you take a stand for God, your faith gets strong. These three Hebrews took a stand for God. They answered the king, "We're not careful to answer you, O King, because we know our God!"

At this point, it seemed like the enemy had won, even though these men were bravely standing for God. It looked like the enemy was going to take advantage of them even though they were committed to God.

But evidently they'd been taught that with God on their side, they could always be winners. According to the circumstances, they sure weren't winners! In fact, it looked like they were utterly defeated. I mean, here they were bound and thrown into a fiery furnace.

DANIEL 3:20-23
20 And he [the king] **commanded the most mighty men that were in his army to bind Shadrach, Meshach, and Abed-nego, and to cast them into the burning fiery furnace.**
21 Then these men were bound in their coats, their hosen, and their hats, and their other

garments, and were cast into the midst of the burning fiery furnace.
22 Therefore because the king's commandment was urgent, and the furnace exceeding hot, the flame of the fire slew those men that took up Shadrach, Meshach, and Abed-nego.
23 And these three men, Shadrach, Meshach, and Abed-nego, fell down bound into the midst of the burning fiery furnace.

Now let me ask you a question. Doesn't that look like defeat to you? Even though the Hebrews boasted loud and strong, "God is going to deliver us," all they got for it was a hot oven!

If it had been some of us, when we didn't get delivered like *we* had it all planned out, we would have been crying to God, "Oh, Lord! My hands are bound, and I'm about to be thrown into this fiery furnace. And here I thought You were going to deliver me!"

It will take a greater commitment of faith than that if you're going to be delivered. You're going to have to stand steadfastly on the Word and believe God for your deliverance. In fact, where there's no commitment to believing God, there's no strong faith!

I want you to see something about a strong commitment to faith in God.

Yes, these Hebrews were thrown into the fire, all right. But the only thing that happened to them is the fire burned off the ropes that had them bound!

How do I know that? Because when the king looked into the fiery furnace, he saw the Hebrews walking around free!

What you need to understand is that sometimes even though it seems like Satan binds you up and throws you in the middle of the fire, you can still walk free in God. To do that, you'll have to keep on believing God. And if you'll keep your faith in God, God will use that fiery trial to burn off what's binding you!

God can turn your situation around even in the midst of the fire! There's nothing that's too hard for Him. These Hebrew young men didn't throw away their belief in God when they were thrown into that fiery furnace. Their faith in God was strong. That's why they could snatch victory from defeat!

It's not too late for you to snatch victory from defeat in your situation either. If you'll keep your faith in God, all the fire will do is burn off your bonds and turn you loose to get strong in God. Then you can walk around in the fire with God in an atmosphere that is pure Heaven!

The secret to snatching victory from defeat is to fellowship with God in the midst of a fiery trial. That's how you can come out of that ordeal feeling cool and refreshed, even though you've been in the midst of the fire!

DANIEL 3:24,25
24 Then Nebuchadnezzar the king was astonied, and rose up in haste, and spake, and said unto his counsellors, DID NOT WE CAST THREE MEN BOUND INTO THE MIDST OF THE FIRE? They answered and said unto the king, True, O king.
25 He answered and said, Lo, I SEE FOUR MEN LOOSE, WALKING IN THE MIDST OF THE FIRE,

and they have no hurt; and THE FORM OF THE FOURTH IS LIKE THE SON OF GOD.

When those three Hebrew children were walking around in those flames, the king looked into that furnace, and said, "Hey! What's going on! Why are there four men walking around? I thought we threw *three* men in there!"

Then one of his attendants answered, "That's right! We only threw three men into the flames" (v. 25).

Even that heathen king had more sense than some Christians today! At least he could recognize that one of those in that fiery furnace was as the form of the Son of God.

Some of us today are standing in faith, all right. But then we get in the fire and we're so concerned about getting burned, we can't even discern that God is with us! Yet just the day before, we were shouting, "Oh, God will never leave me! His Word says He'll never forsake me. Whoo! Hallelujah!"

Then we get in a situation that seems like a fiery trial, and we start shouting something different. "Oh, God! Why did You forsake me! Where are You? Aren't You going to deliver me?"

Now I want you to notice something else. The three Hebrew children walked around in that fire, and they didn't even bother to try to get out.

I believe they were so covered and protected by an invisible shield of God's glory all around them that the fire and the affliction didn't even touch them or bother them.

That's the way it should be with us when we go through a fiery trial. We should be so saturated with the Presence of God that we're more aware of God than we are the trial!

Those Hebrews must have been perfectly at ease, because they didn't even attempt to get out of that fiery blaze until the king finally said, "Hey, you guys in there! Come out!"

Many Christians today would have run right out of that fire the minute their bonds were loosened. But when the Spirit of God is with you as your Comforter and Helper, you can think that you're right in the middle of Heaven instead of in the midst of the fire!

These Hebrews knew the secret of snatching victory from defeat! They kept their faith in God strong so the devil couldn't win in the end. Some of us need to remember that!

The devil tries to do the same sort of thing to us today. He tries to throw us into a fiery trial. Then he'll taunt us to get us out of faith. He'll tell us his lies by saying things like, "All the miracles of God have been done away with. God's mighty acts of wonders are no more. God isn't going to deliver you! If you try to believe Him for this miracle, you'll just die."

Don't you fall for the enemy's lies! God is the same today as He was in the days of the three Hebrew children. His arm is not shortened! Since God could save and deliver those Hebrews, He can save and deliver you and me!

But you need to know that when you take a stand
for the Word of God, sometimes you're going to be
ridiculed. Some people are going to laugh at you and
say, "You can't be so simple-minded that you believe
there's a God!"

Or they'll say things like, "You can't be so stupid as
to actually believe you can be healed. Why, healing was
done away with a long time ago!

Or they'll say, "You can't be so simple-minded as to
believe that God wants to prosper you. Don't you know
prosperity won't work for today?" Sometimes they'll
even say things like, "God is sovereign, so He doesn't
have to do anything for us today. He can do whatever
He wants to do, so you may not get your healing this
time."

Yes, it's true that God is sovereign. He can do what
He wants to do. But what they don't tell you is that God
will not violate His Word. He won't go contrary to what
He's already said! If God didn't honor His Word, He'd be
a liar. The Bible says, "God is not a liar." And what God
says in His Word, He will perform for you and me
because God never changes.

NUMBERS 23:19
19 GOD IS NOT A MAN, THAT HE SHOULD LIE;
neither the son of man, that he should repent:
hath he said, and shall he not do it? or hath he
spoken, and shall he not make it good?

God already said in His Word that He established a
healing covenant with mankind whom He made and

fashioned. Healing was *God's* idea, not ours! In fact, God established His healing covenant with Israel back in Exodus chapter 15, and it hasn't changed to this day. And it will not change until Jesus comes again and we receive our glorified bodies.

Also, in His Word, God said that He wanted to prosper us and give us the blessings of Abraham (Gal. 3:13,14,29). Some will say, "Oh, you can't be simple enough to believe that! The only blessing you're going to get in this life is what you make for yourself, so you might as well get out there and cheat and lie, so you can get all you can!"

Friend, that's the way of the world! The world will tell you, "Tell a half-truth if it's going to make you a dollar." That may bring success according to the world's standards, but it will never bring success with God!

Walk close to God so you can snatch victory from defeat! You can preach faith, all right, but you've still got to live right. However, you've got to realize that when you make a strong commitment to live for God, you're going to face some opposition.

Just know that when you're standing in faith for something you're believing God for, Satan will try to oppose you. Your faith may be tested in the fire. But don't lose your faith! Don't get upset if God doesn't deliver you exactly the way you thought He should.

Maybe you thought He should have delivered you *before* you were actually thrown into the fire! But if you'll just learn how to snatch victory from defeat, it doesn't matter *when* God delivers you, you can know your deliverance is certain!

Stand in faith believing God, and the fire won't hurt you. You'll walk out of that fiery ordeal unharmed. By faith in God, you'll snatch victory from utter defeat! Hallelujah!

Come Forth Into Victory!

In John 11 we find another example of God's snatching victory from defeat. Jesus' friend Lazarus had died. Jesus came to Martha and Mary after Lazarus had been dead four days.

Martha said, "Oh, Jesus! If You had been here four days ago, Lazarus wouldn't have died."

Everyone was crying and carrying on. Jesus said, "Only believe." Then He went to the grave where they'd laid Lazarus. Jesus told those standing by, "Roll away the stone."

JOHN 11:39-44
39 Jesus said, Take ye away the stone. Martha, the sister of him that was dead, saith unto him, Lord, by this time he stinketh: for he hath been dead four days.
40 Jesus saith unto her, Said I not unto thee, that, IF THOU WOULDEST BELIEVE, THOU SHOULDEST SEE THE GLORY OF GOD?
41 Then they took away the stone from the place where the dead was laid. And Jesus lifted up his eyes, and said, Father, I thank thee that thou hast heard me.
42 And I knew that thou hearest me always: but because of the people which stand by I said it, that they may believe that thou hast sent me.

43 And when he thus had spoken, he cried with a loud voice, Lazarus, COME FORTH.
44 And he that was dead came forth, bound hand and foot with graveclothes: and his face was bound about with a napkin. Jesus saith unto them, LOOSE HIM, AND LET HIM GO.

Out of utter defeat, Jesus Christ brought forth victory. As Jesus stepped up to the mouth of that grave, He cried out, "Lazarus! Wake up and come forth!"

Lazarus came hopping out because he was still all bound up in those grave clothes. Jesus said, "Loose him and let him go."

By His power, God caused victory to spring out of utter defeat! Sometimes out of the ashes of disappointment can come forth the greatest victory *if* we'll just believe God. Sometimes we think we've failed and that everything has been destroyed. But if we'll just look to God, He can raise us up so our lives can shine to His glory.

Maybe you feel like you've been bound with grave clothes. Well, what Jesus did for Lazarus, He can do for you. Maybe the devil has come in and tried to destroy everything you've got. Maybe he tried to take you under, and it looks like you're finished.

But if you'll keep your faith in God, God can come along, and out of the rubble and the heap of those ashes, He can raise you to newness of life. By snatching victory out of defeat, you can once again walk in triumph.

It's time that we understood that just because we're
in the midst of an affliction or some terrible storm of
life, fiery furnace, or lions' den — God is still *God!* Tests
and trials are no sign God has forsaken us. If we'll just
keep believing God, we'll come out on the other side,
snatching victory out of defeat every single time.

The Storms of Life

We find another instance of a great man of faith
snatching victory out of defeat because he held on to his
faith in God. In Acts 27, Paul had advised the owners of
the ship that sailing at that particular time would be
dangerous, but they didn't believe him. So they set sail,
even though Paul warned them against it.

Finally a terrible storm arose and it looked like
everyone on the ship was going to perish. There was no
hope. Everything looked black and bleak and hopeless.
There was little chance of survival, and it looked like
the ship was going to be destroyed.

ACTS 27:9-25
**9 Now when much time was spent, and when
sailing was now dangerous, because the fast was
now already past, Paul admonished them,
10 And said unto them, Sirs, I perceive that this
voyage will be with hurt and much damage, not
only of the lading and ship, but also of our lives.
11 Nevertheless the centurion believed the master
and the owner of the ship, more than those things
which were spoken by Paul.
12 And because the haven was not commodious to
winter in, the more part advised to depart thence**

also, if by any means they might attain to Phenice, and there to winter. . . .

13 And when the south wind blew softly, supposing that they had obtained their purpose, loosing thence, they sailed close by Crete.

14 But not long after there arose against it a tempestuous wind, called Euroclydon.

15 And when the ship was caught, and could not bear up into the wind, we let her drive.

16 And running under a certain island which is called Clauda, we had much work to come by the boat:

17 Which when they had taken up, they used helps, undergirding the ship; and, fearing lest they should fall into the quicksands, strake sail, and so were driven.

18 And we being exceedingly tossed with a tempest, the next day they lightened the ship;

19 And the third day we cast out with our own hands the tackling of the ship.

20 And when neither sun nor stars in many days appeared, and no small tempest lay on us, all hope that we should be saved was then taken away.

21 But after long abstinence Paul stood forth in the midst of them, and said, Sirs, ye should have hearkened unto me, and not have loosed from Crete, and to have gained this harm and loss.

22 And now I exhort you to be of good cheer: for there shall be no loss of any man's life among you, but of the ship.

23 For there stood by me this night the angel of God, whose I am, and whom I serve,

24 Saying, Fear not, Paul; thou must be brought before Caesar: and, lo, God hath given thee all them that sail with thee.

25 Wherefore, sirs, be of good cheer: FOR I BELIEVE GOD, THAT IT SHALL BE EVEN AS IT WAS TOLD ME.

The sailors did everything they could to try to keep the ship together. They even tied ropes around the ship to try to keep it together. The crew threw everything overboard that wasn't absolutely necessary, and they even started tearing the gear loose from the deck to throw that overboard.

That ship was pitching and rolling in the storm, and it was about to go under. It was a desperate situation! All hope was gone.

Have you ever been in a water craft in the midst of a violent storm when you had no control over the ship? The ship is tossing and turning and running wild with the wind. That's worse than trying to drive an 18-wheel semitruck without brakes!

You don't have any way of controlling a ship that's just running with the wind in a raging storm. The sailors could see the reef getting closer and closer as the ship was driven pell-mell by the storm toward those jagged rocks.

Every member of that crew was in peril of their lives. They were headed for utter destruction because that ship was going to be smashed on the reefs.

What did Paul do? Did he panic? Did he lose his faith in God? No! In the midst of this hopelessness, Paul stood up tall in God. He stood his ground on the Word of the Lord to him. In the midst of the storm, Paul stood on the deck of that ship and he said, "Wherefore, sirs, *I believe God*" (Acts 27:25).

Think about what Paul must have gone through. The wind was howling, and the ship was being driven violently to and fro by the wind. The boat eventually broke into pieces, but no one's life was lost because God is faithful to His Word. Paul snatched victory from defeat.

Faith *Expects* Victory

Can you stand strong in faith on the deck of *your* ship when the storms of life are tossing *you* to and fro? Can you declare, "I believe God! I believe God's Word that it shall be even as it was told me!"

In the midst of certain destruction, Paul declared his faith in God: "Sirs, I believe that it will be even as it was told me."

That's what you've got to do! You've got to believe what God has told you, in spite of what your circumstances are telling you! You've got to proclaim your faith in God even when it looks like your ship is going down for the last time on the sea of life's circumstances.

If you feel battered and torn apart by the storms of life, that's the time to declare your faith in God. That's the time to know that God has a victory plan for you, and that you *can* snatch victory from certain defeat!

When everything looks like utter destruction, that's when you need to plant your foot on the bow of your ship and stand your ground proclaiming, "I believe that it will be even as it has been told me.

"No weapon formed against me shall prosper. No harm shall come nigh me! No plague shall overtake my dwelling."

Snatch victory from defeat. Oh, glory to God! Nothing is impossible with God! You can do it because you have the Word of God to put you over and the Greater One living on the inside of you. God knows His plans for you, and they are plans for *victory*, not plans for failure and defeat!

Jesus Our Champion
Snatched Victory From Defeat!

Of course, of all the accounts in the Word, the greatest Man of faith of all time who snatched victory from defeat is Jesus Christ, the Son of God. Jesus Christ stood falsely accused and sentenced to death. As Jesus hung upon the Cross of Calvary, He breathed His last breath, and said, "It is finished!" He gave up the ghost and died.

When Jesus was taken down from that Cross and put in the grave, it was a dark day. All hope was lost. In their despair, the disciples scattered like sheep without a shepherd. They were afraid they might be found and tried also. That's why Peter denied Jesus (Matt. 26:74).

Apparently defeated, the Son of God — Jesus Christ the Anointed One — stood all alone. He'd led a sinless life. Everywhere He went, He did good by healing and delivering the people.

This was the same Jesus who had stood on the boat on the Sea of Galilee and commanded, "Peace, be still!" and the winds and waves obeyed Him. Now He stood alone and forsaken, rejected of men.

This was the same Jesus who stood among the tombs and cast the devils out of the Gadarene demoniac. Even devils feared Him! This was Jesus, the matchless Son of God, who had ridden into Jerusalem in victory on a donkey. The crowds sang His praises: "Hosanna! Hosanna in the Highest!" Those same crowds now yelled, "Crucify Him!"

"Give us Barabbas," they cried. "Crucify Jesus! We don't want Him to be our king. Caesar is our king!"

So Jesus was laid crucified and dead in the tomb. All was lost. The Kingdom that He preached about establishing seemed forgotten and impossible of fulfillment. Those who did remember His words about His Kingdom, said, "Well, I guess it's not going to happen. He failed us."

But on that third day, God snatched victory from utter defeat as Jesus Christ rose and ascended on High to sit and reign in glory at the Father's right hand. Yes, Jesus did establish His Kingdom — His spiritual Kingdom among believers. He is the greatest Man of faith of all time!

There was no defeat for Jesus! God snatched the supreme victory from the ultimate defeat! We are now waiting for that day when the trump of God shall sound, and Jesus will come back and set up His literal Kingdom. But until then, we can go on rejoicing, knowing that there is no real defeat as long as we stay in Him!

Oh, sometimes it might look like defeat. It might even smell like defeat! It might seem like defeat all around. But there's no defeat as long as you abide in Jesus.

I don't know about you, but I am determined that I shall stand and proclaim that I will snatch victory from defeat every time. As long as my feet are planted firmly on God's Word, the devil cannot defeat me. And I will not quit!

I want to encourage you to enter into God's victory plan for your life no matter what kind of battle you're in. It doesn't matter what you're facing, God is able to cause you to snatch victory from defeat. God's victory belongs to you!

Your Heavenly Father can take every test or trial in your life right now and turn it around. God's victory plan can't fail if you'll just abide in His Word and believe Him. You just have to stay in His plan.

Learn to snatch victory from defeat. How? Learn to look at every setback in your life, not as defeat, but as an opportunity for God to show Himself strong in your behalf. Ask God to demonstrate His power to you, and He will show you that He is still God!

Chapter 7
What Comes After Victory?

It's important to talk about down-to-earth subjects that everyone faces in life. Practical faith subjects like how to receive answers to prayer help us in our everyday life because they help us accomplish everything God has for us.

But it's also important to know what to do *after* we win great victories in God, because so many times that's when Satan will try to set up roadblocks in our lives.

Of course, everyone likes to talk about victory and success and how to receive from God. But we don't hear people talk too much about what to do after great victories to protect ourselves from the devil's schemes. However, there are some important lessons we must learn if we're going to stand strong in God *after* the victory too.

You know, it's easy to sing and shout when you've experienced a major triumph. If you receive a victory of healing or if a financial need is met, you rejoice. You're just so excited about what God has done for you that you want to run and jump and tell everyone about it and have a great time.

But what happens after all the excitement has died down? What do you do after the crowd has all gone home, and your friends aren't there anymore to rejoice with you?

When we're at church and God meets our needs, it's easy to rejoice with our friends and have a high time in the Lord! But after that, sometimes when we go home and we're alone, there's a letdown from all the excitement. That's when the devil tries to come in and attack us. Have you ever had that happen?

I've heard an old saying paraphrased many times. It goes like this: "Let us be as watchful *after* the victory as *before* the battle." That's a good statement because it tells us to be forewarned and forearmed against the devil's strategies.

We've also heard it said that life is not a playground; it's a battleground. And when we look at this statement from a spiritual standpoint, we see in the Word of God that this is the truth. The Bible says we wrestle and that we are in a spiritual warfare (Eph. 6:12-18).

The Word of God uses all those terms to describe our walk down here on this earth. It tells us that we have to fight the good fight of *faith*. We have to keep the shield of faith raised high to protect us from the evil one.

We know Satan is going to try to hinder us, but many times we don't know exactly *how* he's going to do it. If we knew exactly how he was going to hinder us, we would block him before he ever got to us.

I mean, you'd be stupid to just sit there and watch him come into your house and attack you or your family. If you knew a thief was going to try to break into your house and rob you by slipping in the back door, you'd be foolish not to try to do something to keep him out.

If you knew an arsonist was coming down your street, would you just sit on your front porch and watch him walk up to your house? If he set fire to the houses on both sides of your house and then headed for your driveway, would you just sit there and let him set fire to *your* house? Of course not!

But that's what some believers do with the devil! They just sit there and do nothing and let Satan come in and devour their homes and their lives.

If we don't take authority over the devil, that's exactly what we're doing — we're just letting the devil come in and take over!

Most of the time, we are on guard against Satan, so he has to slip in like a thief. One way he sneaks in is by finding our weak point. He finds the place in our lives that we're not guarding so he can take us unawares.

The Word Guards Your Life

We need to be careful to guard our lives with the Word of God and prayer. How do we do that?

Well, for example, when I was growing up, there were two or three different groups of kids that always played together. We each had our own fort or clubhouse. We'd set guards or sentries around the clubhouse to make sure that the other kids didn't slip in on us.

When I was in the army, we'd do the same thing in some of our military exercises. We'd post sentries around the parameters of our area to keep the enemy from coming in and attacking us. The sentries also gave us advance warning.

Well, the Word of God is your sentry. It's your defense against the enemy. If you'll walk in the promises of God, you'll be safe from falling prey to the enemy's devices.

1 PETER 5:8
8 Be sober, be vigilant; because your adversary the devil, as a roaring lion, walketh about, SEEKING WHOM HE MAY DEVOUR.

You've got to be alert and abiding in the Word if you're going to be able to detect the enemy trying to slip in unawares. The devil prowls around like a roaring lion trying to devour you.

The Bible compares him to a roaring lion because if he catches you off guard, he can be that ferocious. The Bible also says Satan will try to come in like a deceiving spirit. In other words, he's sneaky.

2 CORINTHIANS 11:13,14
13 For such are false apostles, deceitful workers, transforming themselves into the apostles of Christ.
14 And no marvel; for SATAN HIMSELF IS TRANSFORMED INTO AN ANGEL OF LIGHT.

One of the times to really be on the lookout for the devil's wiles is after we've won a great victory. Normally when we've been believing God for certain things to come to pass and we finally receive our victory report, we have a tendency to let our guard down (1 Cor. 10:12). And that's exactly when the enemy tries to move in.

We think, *Thank God! It finally happened!* In that time of relief and rejoicing and praising God, the pressure is finally off, and we forget to beware of the enemy that's still roaming around trying to devour us.

Sometimes it's in our times of rejoicing that the enemy will come in and deal us a harsh blow because we're not alert to defend ourselves. The reason we're not alert is that we're too busy rejoicing and having a party because our need has been met, so we let our guard down.

It's great to rejoice and praise God. We're supposed to do that — the Bible says so. But while we're rejoicing, let's set out some sentries, so to speak, to guard our territory so the enemy can't come in and take us unawares. The promises in God's Word are like sentries that guard our lives.

Faith on the Mountaintop — But Failure in the Valley

I think that's what happened to the prophet Elijah. In First Kings 18, we see that Elijah experienced a lapse of faith after a great victory. Evidently he didn't guard himself after his victory on the mountaintop, so the enemy was able to come in to try to devour him. *His lapse of faith started when he began expecting the worst.*

The prophet Elijah went up on Mount Carmel with God and won a tremendous victory against the prophets of Baal.

Elijah stood nonchalantly by while the prophets of Baal cut themselves, trying to get their god to answer them. Elijah mocked them, saying, *". . . Cry aloud: for he is a god; either he is talking, or he is pursuing, or he is in a journey, or peradventure he sleepeth, and must be awaked"* (1 Kings 18:27).

So the prophets of Baal just cried louder and cut themselves some more. Elijah really agitated the prophets of Baal because he was clothed with the power of the Spirit, and he knew that God was going to show Himself mighty on Elijah's behalf.

Then Elijah stepped up to the altar of the Lord that he'd built. He prayed, and the power of God fell like fire, burning up the sacrifice and licking up the water in the trench around it.

The prophets of Baal had prayed and screamed to their god all day long. But Elijah prayed, and probably in less than two minutes, God demonstrated Himself with mighty power. God showed up!

1 KINGS 18:31-38
31 And Elijah took twelve stones, according to the number of the tribes of the sons of Jacob, unto whom the word of the Lord came, saying, Israel shall be thy name:
32 And with the stones he built an altar in the name of the Lord: and he made a trench about the altar. . . .
33 And he put the wood in order, and cut the bullock in pieces, and laid him on the wood, and said,

> Fill four barrels with water, and pour it on the
> burnt sacrifice, and on the wood.
> 34 And he said, Do it the second time. And they
> did it the second time. And he said, Do it the third
> time. And they did it the third time.
> 35 And the water ran round about the altar; and
> he filled the trench also with water.
> 36 And it came to pass at the time of the offering of
> the evening sacrifice, that Elijah the prophet came
> near, and said, Lord God of Abraham, Isaac, and of
> Israel, let it be known this day that thou art God
> in Israel, and that I am thy servant, and that I
> have done all these things at thy word.
> 37 Hear me, O Lord, hear me, that this people may
> know that thou art the Lord God, and that thou
> hast turned their heart back again.
> 38 Then the fire of the Lord fell, and consumed
> the burnt sacrifice, and the wood, and the stones,
> and the dust, and licked up the water that was in
> the trench.

Now here is Elijah, this great man of God, who'd just called fire down from Heaven and watched in triumph as the fire consumed his sacrifice — a sacrifice soaked with *twelve barrels* of water! Then Elijah killed all the prophets of Baal (1 Kings 18:40). Now that's a tremendous victory over the enemy, isn't it!

But when the wicked Queen Jezebel heard what Elijah had done to her prophets, she sent a messenger to tell Elijah, ". . . *let the gods do to me, and more also, if I make not thy life as the life of one of them by tomorrow about this time*" (1 Kings 19:2).

So what did this great man of God do after he heard the queen's threat? Remember, this was the prophet who had just defeated all the prophets of Baal by the power of God! But when he heard Jezebel's threat, he turned and ran in fear.

That reminds me of some Christians. Sometimes right after they've won a tremendous victory, some little trial comes along, and instead of resisting the enemy and standing strong in faith, the first thing they do is turn and run! They cry, "Oh, the devil's been after me. Bless His holy Name."

When I was a kid, it took me the longest time to figure out what some people were talking about when they'd get up and testify in church, "The devil's been after me all day long. Bless His holy Name."

I finally figured out that they weren't trying to bless the *devil*. They were talking about Jesus when they said, "Bless His holy Name." But they sure got their praise misplaced!

Sometimes after you've experienced a great spiritual victory, the devil will hit you with a counterattack, and if you're not on your guard, it can cause you to turn and run.

That's exactly what happened to Elijah. After his great victory, when Jezebel threatened his life, Elijah turned and ran for his life! Now think about it! Elijah had just called down fire out of Heaven, so why should he have been worried about Queen Jezebel?

If God could take care of him on the mountaintop, couldn't He take care of him in the valley? Elijah's problem was that he didn't guard himself after the victory, so he began to expect the worst. Expecting the worst is really expecting Satan to triumph over God!

So Elijah fled to the wilderness and sat down and cried, "Lord, there isn't any reason for me to live anymore! Just take my life."

1 KINGS 19:4
4 But he himself went a day's journey into the wilderness, and came and sat down under a juniper tree: and he requested for himself that he might die; and said, It is enough; now, O Lord, take away my life....

But Elijah didn't really want to die. If he'd wanted to die, he could have just stayed where he was and kept on anticipating the worst! Then he would have died for sure!

On the other hand, Elijah could also have stayed where he was and expected the best. If he'd depended on God to deliver him from wicked Queen Jezebel, he would have walked in God's victory plan for his life. There's no way Jezebel could have touched him!

God would have delivered Elijah if he'd just cried out to God, "Lord Jehovah, God of Abraham, Isaac, and Jacob! I call upon You now for Your protecting power!"

Do you know whose head would have rolled then? Jezebel's! God had His victory plan all figured out. He knew exactly what He was going to do to rescue Elijah.

But instead of staying in faith and expecting the best, Elijah had a lapse of faith and ran away in fear.

He wasn't on guard against the enemy's wiles. He didn't know Satan would try to sneak in to devour him after a great victory. We need to learn from Elijah's experience.

I have seen this same thing happen many times in people's lives. They believed God, and they stood for healing or a financial miracle or some other need to be met. They stood firm in their faith, and they received a great miracle from God.

But after the victory, some of these same people ran for their lives, so to speak, in discouragement and defeat. Have you ever seen that happen to anyone? But that doesn't have to happen if believers will just guard themselves against the wiles of the enemy!

What happens after the victory party is over?

You see, all the people rejoiced on that mountaintop with Elijah when he won that great victory over the prophets of Baal. They all cried out, "Jehovah is God!"

But do you know what? Elijah expected all these people to turn from Baal and start worshipping God, and they didn't. Elijah didn't guard himself from discouragement, so he felt sorry for himself and began to complain to God that he was the only one left to serve God. God told Elijah that there was a remnant of seven thousand who hadn't bowed their knee and worshiped Baal (1 Kings 19:9-18).

There's another lesson in this for *us*. We need to be careful that we don't get overly confident in our victories. We can win many victories for God, but we can also get overly confident in ourselves. We can begin to think, *There's nothing that can overcome me.*

Well, that's true in a sense. There's nothing that can overcome you as long as you stay in God's Word and your faith is in Him! As long as God is doing the work, not *you*, you can't be overcome by the enemy.

It's true that we're overcomers. But we are only overcomers as long as we are in Christ. You see, if we get a boastful attitude, we're in trouble.

You know someone's headed for problems if he brags, "I just defeated the enemy in this trial! Just let him try that again! I'm ready for him!"

There's an element of truth to that, but if you're not careful, you can get to thinking more highly of yourself than you ought. Besides, it wasn't *you* who did anything, anyway. It was Christ who lives in you. Greater is He who is in you than he that's in the world (1 John 4:4).

Anytime you win a faith battle with the enemy, you really didn't overcome the enemy yourself or win the victory in your own strength. You just allowed the Greater One on the inside of you to take control of the situation and win the victory for you. All you did was move out of the way and keep self from ruling in the situation, so the Greater One could do His work.

But in the process of watching God fight your battles for you, you can get taken up with the glory of the victory and get a big head! While you're enjoying the benefits of the victory, just remember who the Greater One is. It's *not* you — it's God!

Really, when we get ourselves out of the way and yield to the Spirit of God and let Him dominate in the situation, the power of God will work wonders for us every single time!

But we can get overly confident in ourselves and in our own strength. It's too easy to get the attitude, *Oh, I put the devil down! It's nothing. I can take care of him.*

Oh, no, you can't! Not in yourself you can't.

It's true that Jesus already defeated the devil, and all you have to do is walk in Jesus' victory plan. You need to have confidence in the authority you have in Christ.

And it's true that you need tenacity to hold on to your victory over Satan. Let him know who is in authority! But you can only do that because you are in Christ Jesus. Jesus is the One who has done the defeating, and you are just reaping the benefits of Jesus' victory.

But it's important that you realize that some of the greatest tests you will ever face will hit you right after you've experienced some of your most tremendous victories. Now think back for a minute. How many of you realize that this has happened to you in the past? You experienced some of your greatest tests just after you experienced great triumphs.

Sometimes I think that tests after great victories show us how much we need to depend on God! At times like that we see just how much we've really learned in our faith walk.

Evidently Elijah hadn't learned anything because he was running scared, even though it was obvious that God had performed a great miracle for him. It was obvious that the prophets of Baal were defeated in the situation. It was obvious that Jehovah God had declared Himself to be the God of gods.

But let me ask you a question. Was the power of God still available to Elijah *after* this great miracle? Could God have saved Elijah from Queen Jezebel? Could the same God who sent fire out of Heaven to consume the sacrifice, protect the prophet of God? Of course! Elijah won the victory, but he didn't learn the lesson.

Many of us have won great victories, but we have never learned the lesson. We keep running back to God wanting Him to create another victory for us. Really, the victories God gives us are to teach us something. We're supposed to learn to rely on the power of God because we're in Christ and not to run from any problem.

God demonstrates His power to us in our victories, so we'll know that the same power is available to us in any situation or problem. But how many of us have learned that lesson? Instead, a lot of us run from the problem like we've never seen the power of God demonstrated in our behalf!

But then on Mount Horeb, Elijah cried and carried on, saying, "Oh, Lord, You might as well just come down here and take me home. Everyone has turned their back on You except me" (1 Kings 19:8-10).

Elijah really got in to a poor-ole-me attitude. Elijah went from the mountain of the mighty demonstration of God's power to the mountain of disillusionment and disappointment. On Mount Carmel, Elijah stood on the mountaintop of God's glory, but on Mount Horeb, all of his weaknesses showed up.

In other words, Elijah went from the mountain of victory to the mountain of despair in a matter of one or two days! Of course, that's never happened to any of us! Actually, I think all of us can relate to that.

But if Elijah had really learned the spiritual lessons he was supposed to from the victory, he would have stood his ground against Queen Jezebel and said, "The same Jehovah God of Abraham, Isaac, and Jacob who manifested His mighty power will protect me and keep me. I don't have to run off and hide!"

But since Elijah did run and hide, God took care of him anyway and showed him another lesson about His mighty protection and power.

What can we learn from Elijah's experience? For one thing, once you're walking in God's victory plan for your life, don't jump out of it. Stay in the victory! To do that, you'll have to guard yourself with the Word in your areas of weakness, so the devil won't take you by surprise. Then you can walk on in faith.

Now I think Elijah eventually learned from this lesson, because we never find him in that position again, at least as it is recorded in the Word of God.

You see, some of us have been shown lesson after lesson after lesson, but we haven't learned from any of them yet. Elijah went to the school of faith and was taught the lesson, but when test time came, he failed the test. He should have known that God's protection overshadowed him.

The Bible says that Elijah was a man subject to like passions just as we are (James 5:17). That means we are made in like manner — we're human just like Elijah. So let's learn from our past victories in God. Then we can profit from the lesson the victory taught us about God's great power so we don't fail the test!

The Disciples' Faith Failure After Great Victories

What about in the New Testament? Are there any believers who experienced a faith failure after achieving great victories? Yes, Jesus' disciples made that same mistake too.

After all, they had been with Jesus throughout His earthly ministry. For example, they were there when Jesus turned the water into wine at the marriage at Cana (John 2:11). They witnessed Jesus heal the lepers and the blind men, and raise the widow's son from the dead. Time and time again they saw Jesus as He ministered to the masses and healed them and set them free.

With their own eyes, the disciples had witnessed the miracle of Jesus feeding five thousand people from a few fish and loaves of bread (Matt. 14:15-21). That was a tremendous victory.

How many people do you know who have experienced such a dramatic miracle? In a sense, the disciples were even a part of that miracle because they helped pass out the loaves of bread and the fish!

I'm sure the multitudes rejoiced as the disciples passed out the bread and the fish. Maybe some of the people in that crowd even patted them on the back and said things like, "Boy, you guys are really something. Man, you're something else!"

But right after this miracle, Jesus told the disciples, "Let's go over to the other side." Jesus and His disciples got into the ship; they were going to cross over the Sea of Galilee to the other side. Then because he was weary from ministering to the multitudes, He fell asleep in the ship. A storm arose, and the disciples got fearful.

Many people think, *Oh, if only I could have lived when Jesus ministered on this earth! I could have followed Him, and I wouldn't have had any troubles at all.*

But I want you to know that Jesus' disciples, the twelve men who lived the closest to Him, faced difficult circumstances even though Jesus was physically present with them! Even though Jesus was with them, they still got fearful.

> **MARK 4:35-40**
> **35 And the same day, when the even was come, he saith unto them, Let us pass over unto the other side.**
> **36 And when they had sent away the multitude, they took him even as he was in the ship. And there were also with him other little ships.**
> **37 And there arose a great storm of wind, and the waves beat into the ship, so that it was now full.**
> **38 And he was in the hinder part of the ship, asleep on a pillow: and they awake him, and say**

**unto him, MASTER, CAREST THOU NOT THAT
WE PERISH?
39 And he arose, and rebuked the wind, and said
unto the sea, Peace, be still. And the wind ceased,
and there was a great calm.
40 And he said unto them, WHY ARE YE SO
FEARFUL? HOW IS IT THAT YE HAVE NO FAITH?**

Let me tell you, circumstances suddenly got rough!
In fact, the disciples thought they were going to perish.
So they awakened Jesus, saying, *". . . Master, carest
thou not that we perish?"* (v. 38).

That reminds me of some of us: "Oh, God! Why did
You let this happen to me? Don't You love me anymore?"

What we fail to realize is that God sees all the trouble we're in before we ever tell Him about it. He wants
to find out what we're going to do in the midst of the
trouble.

Are we going to get fearful and frustrated and begin
to whimper and cry? Or are we going to stand up like
soldiers of faith and walk in God's victory plan for our
lives?

You know the story. Jesus immediately stilled the
storm. But then He turned to the disciples and asked,
". . . Why are ye so fearful? . . ." (Mark 4:40).

Now that sounds like a foolish question, doesn't it?
Can't you just imagine what was going through the disciples' minds? *What do You mean, Why are we so fearful? Can't You see that the waves are up over the top of
the ship! Can't You see that we're about to capsize?
That's why we're fearful!*

You know, if it had been us, most of us would have said, "What are You talking about, Lord? Don't You see those huge waves about ready to crash in upon us? Lord, why don't You do something about it?"

But when Jesus asked them, "Why are you so fearful?" He was dealing with a much deeper issue here. He was trying to get the disciples to see that when their faith is anchored in God and in His Word, there is no room for fear.

The entrance of God's Word gives light (Ps. 119:130). Where light is, the spirit of fear must depart.

Instead of leaning on Jesus, the living Word of God, the disciples were ready to let go of their faith and get into fear. Their problem was that they did not really believe what Jesus had said. He said, "Let's go to the other side," *not* "Let's go part way across the sea, but we won't make it!"

In the past, the disciples had seen what happened when Jesus spoke. People were healed, the dead were raised, miracles were performed. But even though the disciples had witnessed all those miracles, when the difficulties of life came, they didn't lean on Jesus' words.

The disciples had seen that *whatever* Jesus said, came to pass. They saw Him when He cursed the fig tree and it withered from the root (Matt. 21:19-21). Yet they actually had more faith in their circumstances than they did in Jesus' words! No wonder Jesus asked them, "Where is your faith?"

That's no way to walk in God's victory plan! Jesus
had a plan. He knew ahead of time what He wanted to
accomplish on the other side of that sea. All the disciples had to do was trust in Jesus' word, "Let us go over
to the other side."

When Jesus asked them, "Where is your faith?" He
was really asking, "What in the world are you afraid of?
You've seen the power of God in demonstration! Yet you
so quickly took your eyes off My Word to you and looked
at the circumstances."

We sometimes make the same mistake the disciples
did. We can start out walking in God's victory plan for
our lives. We're living right. We're making all the right
confessions. We're obeying the Word of God. We're doing
all we know to do. But when the storms of life come
against us like they did for the disciples, we've still got
to keep on looking at God.

The minute we look at the boisterous winds of the
tests and trials, we're going to fail. That's exactly what
happened to Peter. He'd witnessed Jesus' great miracles. He knew the power of God because he'd been an
eyewitness to most of Jesus' works of power.

Peter had a lot of faith during the miraculous
events of Jesus' ministry. But it wasn't long before
Peter was tested in his faith. The minute he took his
eyes off God, he played right into the hand of the
enemy.

MATTHEW 14:22-31
22 And straightway Jesus constrained his disci-
ples to get into a ship, and to go before him unto
the other side, while he sent the multitudes away.

23 And when he had sent the multitudes away, he went up into a mountain apart to pray: and when the evening was come, he was there alone.
24 But the ship was now in the midst of the sea, tossed with waves: for the wind was contrary.
25 And in the fourth watch of the night Jesus went unto them, walking on the sea.
26 And when the disciples saw him walking on the sea, they were troubled, saying, It is a spirit; and they cried out for fear.
27 But straightway Jesus spake unto them, saying, Be of good cheer; it is I; be not afraid.
28 And Peter answered him and said, Lord, if it be thou, bid me come unto thee on the water.
29 And he said, Come. And when Peter was come down out of the ship, he walked on the water, to go to Jesus.
30 But WHEN HE SAW THE WIND BOISTEROUS, he was afraid; and beginning to sink, he cried, saying, Lord, save me.
31 And immediately Jesus stretched forth his hand, and caught him, and said unto him, O thou of little faith, wherefore didst thou doubt?

Peter asked Jesus, "Lord, if it's really You, let me come to You on the water."

Jesus answered, "Come on."

Peter stepped out of the boat and began to walk on the water. But when he started looking at the circumstances surrounding him, he began to sink.

The Lord in His mercy reached out and grabbed Peter, or he would have drowned. But before we criticize Peter too harshly, we need to realize that at least he got out of the boat and took a few steps in faith before he fell!

Some of us have never even gotten out of the boat! So let's not criticize Peter until we get out of the boat and try to do something for God!

I would ask you the same question Jesus asked His disciples. Where is your faith? Is it in God's Word? Or is it in the ability of your circumstances to totally overwhelm you?

If you really have faith in God's Word, it will serve as a reassuring anchor in the midst of any storm or any crisis. No matter how high those waves try to crash round about you, if you trust God, He will deliver you!

When you trust God, it becomes His responsibility to see that you are delivered. When you rest your faith entirely on Him, there is no such word as impossible. Jesus said, ". . . *If thou canst believe, all things are possible to him that believeth*" (Mark 9:23). He also said, ". . . *The things which are impossible with men are possible with God*" (Luke 18:27).

Each one of us needs to learn the lesson the disciples eventually learned. I believe Elijah learned it too. Right after experiencing a great victory is no time to let our guard down. We've got to keep on fighting the good fight of faith, because as long as we're on this earth, the enemy is going to keep on trying to defeat us!

But thank God, God and His Word can be depended on. There is no test, trial, or circumstance that is too hard for Him. If we'll look to God's Word, in every situation we'll come out the victor and fulfill God's plan of victory for our lives.

That's what the great men and women of faith in the Bible did. They each found out what God's victory plan was for them, and then they followed that plan exactly. And God was faithful to show Himself strong on their behalf as they trusted Him to deliver them from every fiery trial that came their way.

God's victory plan always prevailed for those who walked in faith and obedience to Him. The thick walls of Jericho tumbled down, the mighty Red Sea parted, lions' mouths were supernaturally shut, and the fiery furnace had no power to burn — all because God's people determined that they would walk in God's victory plan for their lives, no matter what!

The same is true for us. It will be easy to walk in God's victory plan for our lives if we'll just hide His Word in our hearts and walk in obedience to Him. But we have to make the choice every day to seek God for His plan of victory and then follow that plan exactly.

Victory or defeat? Death or deliverance? The choice is ours!

How about you? Are you going to follow God's plan of victory for *you*? Only you can determine whether you will be a victim or a victor, a faith failure or a faith giant. Take your place in Heaven's "Hall of Faith," along with Moses, Joshua, Daniel, and the three Hebrew children. You *can* walk in God's victory plan for your life!